GARDENING FOR
BEGINNERS

GEOFF HAMILTON

BBC BOOKS

Published by BBC Books
A division of BBC Enterprises Ltd
Woodlands, 80 Wood Lane, London W12 0TT

First published 1990

© Geoff Hamilton 1990

ISBN 0 563 36003 8

Drawings by Lindsay Blow
Garden designs by Carol Kurrein

Typeset in Aster by Ace Filmsetting Ltd, Frome
Cover printed by Richard Clay Ltd, Norwich
Printed and bound in Great Britain by Redwood Press Ltd, Melksham

CONTENTS

INTRODUCTION

You may not have realised it yet, but if you're reading this book you're about to embark on one of the most exciting and enduring adventures on offer.

Oh yes, I am fully aware that gardening has the image of being boring and fit only for grandads in greasy waistcoats with string round their trousers, but having spent my whole life gardening I'm also aware what a load of well-rotted manure that image is!

Just imagine it. Here you have an opportunity, every year, of actually creating *life*! You start with a tiny, dry bit of brown nothingness and you finish with a beautiful flowering plant or a plate of the most delicious veg. you've ever tasted. And if you don't get excited over that prospect – well, all I can say is you need a blood transfusion!

Gardening is not only an adventure, it's a mystery too. You'll find that the more you do, the more you begin to understand just what makes nature tick. All the time you'll be subconsciously storing away bits of experience and information that eventually click into place to make you an ace gardener.

But don't expect to learn it all at once. This book certainly won't reveal all the secrets any more than any other. I've been gardening now for thirty-five years and I reckon I'm just beginning to get a grip of it! What is needed is experience.

So, if you've just acquired a new garden for the first time, this is what I suggest you do. Use *Gardening For Beginners* as a starting point, read it and refer to it constantly, but don't rush into doing the whole garden all at once. First make use of other gardeners' experience.

In the first year set yourself a target of perhaps a third of the garden – whatever size it may be. Perhaps you could get the patio done, or lay the lawn and cultivate just one small border. The rest can usefully be put down to grass or, if it's weedy, to potatoes which'll clear the ground and help the budget too.

Then spend that first year visiting as many gardens, nurseries and garden centres as you can. There are hundreds of good gardens open to the public throughout the year, which are a wonderful source of inspiration. Of course, you'll never want to recreate Blenheim Palace or Sissinghurst, I realise that. But even in these massive, stately-home gardens, you'll find plants and little corners of borders that will give you ideas and inspiration for your own.

Be sure to take your notebook on all these visits because, like it or not, you'll find most of the plants labelled in Latin. But don't ever let Latin names turn you off or frighten you to death. I'm being absolutely honest when I say that once you get into the habit of remembering a few, they soon start to become easy. What's more, Latin is such a descriptive and logical language that before long you'll find yourself recognising words and actually knowing what the plant will look like before you even see it! And the look on the face of your neighbour when you tell him or her that this holly is *Ilex altaclarensis* 'Camelliifolia Variegata' makes all that learning well worthwhile!

You'll find, too, that once you start serious gardening, you'll make all kinds of new friends. People at work will bring in plants and seeds and neighbouring gardeners will offer help. They always do.

All I ask is that you enter into your new pastime wholeheartedly and with enthusiasm for just three months. Because I know jolly well that if you give it that kind of chance, however 'boring' you may once have thought it, you'll get hooked in exactly the same way I did thirty-five years ago. Good luck!

GEOFF HAMILTON

CHAPTER 1

GARDEN DESIGN

Designing your first garden is a stimulating experience! It will certainly give you a few head-scratching hours and you'll change your mind a dozen times before you get it right. But it's a rare chance to create a work of art that's entirely your own. What's more, it is guaranteed success, since nature will take a leading role, whether you like it or not. And nature *always* gets it right!

The point to remember about garden design, of course, is that it's a very personal thing. It's your garden, which you will live with for the foreseeable future, so if *you* like what you create, that's all that matters.

That cardinal rule means, of course, that it's difficult, if not impossible, to advise anyone else on how to design their garden. What we can do is show you a few tricks of the trade which will make your task a lot easier and could save a bit of heartache. There are ten main points to consider.

Top Ten Tips

1 The Aspect

All you have to do here is observe your garden, trying to ignore for the moment any builders' rubble or chest-high vegetation. First and foremost find out the degree to which your garden gets the sun, making a mental note at this stage of any areas that remain in permanent shade or are sunny for only short periods.

This will largely depend on whether your garden faces roughly due north (and so is in shade all day), south (sunny all day), east (sunny in the morning) or west (sunny in the late afternoon/evening). At least, that's the theory. In practice, that south-facing garden might never see the sun, thanks to neighbouring trees, houses, or even an office block or two!

How much sun your garden receives (and at what time of day) will be a major factor when it comes to choosing and positioning plants. It will also help to determine the best site for permanent features such as a patio or ornamental pool.

It's a good idea, too, to establish whether or not your garden is exposed to winds that might prove damaging (to plants) or disagreeable (to you). If it is, you can opt to make the provision of windbreaks a major priority (see tip number 8 – Placing of permanent features).

2 The ground

When designing a garden from scratch, try to think of the ground as a painter's empty canvas. OK, so that might require a fair stretch of the imagination at the moment, but it's something to aim for!

You may have inherited a veritable jungle, of course, in which case the bulk of the vegetation will have to be completely cleared (see tip number 3 – Existing features). Alternatively, if you're lucky, you'll have a bare plot relieved only by a bit of building debris and, perhaps, something passing for a patio.

Good ground preparation is the key to a successful garden (see Chapter 2). You should also be prepared to carry out the following essential work, should it be necessary:

- Removal of all rubble, old roots, weeds and so on (they'll haunt you forever if you don't get rid of them!);
- Levelling of an uneven site;
- Terracing of a slope (hard work, admittedly, but without it a steeply sloping garden will be difficult to manage and virtually unusable).

3 Existing features

Take a long, hard look at what you *have* got. In an inherited garden, don't be too keen to uproot existing vegetation as you might find you have some really worthwhile plants lurking in the undergrowth. If you can bear it, live with your garden for the best part of one growing season – say, from April to October – and – who knows? – those borders might become alive with a blaze of spring bulbs or that rather dull-looking bush might burst into bloom bringing autumn colour.

Think twice, too, before you get rid of any sizeable trees (and check with the local council in case they're subject to a preservation order) and mature shrubs. They might not be particularly to your liking, but at least they will help to give the impression that your 'new' garden is well established. Also consider whether such plants are serving a particular purpose – for example, screening an ugly view, providing shelter from wind or making the garden more private.

Assess the merits of all existing features, bearing in mind ways in which they might be improved and accommodated in your garden design. A dilapidated or ill-placed shed, say, could be renovated, moved or hidden with decorative screening. An uninspiring or cracked concrete path could be given a facelift with a brick edging or by repairs to the surface – you could even lay paving over the top.

Remember that all such permanent features will not only be a real chore to remove, but also costly and time-consuming to replace. It makes sense, therefore, to try to make them work to your advantage.

The same goes for existing features outside your plot, especially in the brand-new garden. Note any attractive views – perhaps a neighbour's tree, a rooftop weathervane or distant church spire – and also any eyesores. You can then plan your plantings and position any permanent structures so that they highlight the good points and camouflage the bad.

4 Forward planning

Gardens can be used and enjoyed in a variety of ways, so it's important to establish the role, or roles, you want yours to perform. To this end, consider your priorities so that you can plan accordingly. The following table illustrates the main options available, although it is possible to allow these to overlap and reach a happy compromise:

Priorities	Options	Description	Comments
To keep time spent on gardening to a minimum	Low-maintenance garden	Extensive use of hard surfacing materials; plantings restricted to easy-going shrubs	Initial high construction costs but pays off long-term
To have space to raise a wide variety of plants, etc.	Traditional, ornamental garden	Emphasis on well-shaped and planned borders and allocation of space for crops	Will take time to look established, but is rewarding
To keep the kids happy and the parents free of worry	Practical family garden	Hard surfaces kept to a minimum; tough, easy-going plantings; safe areas for play/equipment	With careful planning, the garden needn't look a mess!
To have a place to relax in and entertain friends, etc.	Leisure garden	Special attention to providing shelter/privacy. Ample patio for furniture, barbecue, etc.	Garden should include focal points – e.g., a pool/fountain

FIRST-TIME BUYER'S GARDEN

cold frame   compost bins

shed

ornamental kitchen garden

border

border

pergola

border

lawn

border

gravel and paving

border

border

patio

Approx. size: 6.5 m (22 ft) × 13 m (42 ft)

5 Dividing the space

As already indicated, the proportion of space you allocate to a partic-ular feature – lawn, borders, patio, vegetable plot and so on – will be determined to a large extent by the way in which your garden is to be used. But the scale of the individual elements also has to be consid-ered in relation to the garden as a whole.

Lawns and borders: In the traditional, ornamental garden, an uncluttered, well-kept expanse of lawn provides a perfect contrast to vibrant, busy borders. In smaller gardens, making the borders too deep might leave you with a pocket-handkerchief of a lawn and the desired effect would be lost. Of course, in a tiny space a lawn is by no means necessary, but if you do include one, aim to have at least two thirds of the garden laid to lawn and the remainder devoted to plants.

Patios: When deciding how big a patio should be, take into account what you are going to do on it and how many people it is going to have to accommodate. You have only to look at the average dining room to see how much space is required to seat a family or friends around a table in reasonable comfort.

You might also want room for a barbecue or sandpit and, certainly, you will want to leave some space for plants. So, if a patio is a priority, be as generous as possible with the proportions. And if that means you are left with only a scrap of space to devote to a lawn, think about using hard materials throughout, dispensing with grass altogether.

Kitchen gardens: If the raising of crops is a major priority, you will probably be happy to sacrifice space elsewhere in the garden in order to have a reasonable-sized plot – in any case, it's likely to keep you far too busy to laze around on a patio! However, if your garden is quite small and you don't want it to look like an allotment, consider grow-ing crops in conventional borders alongside your ornamental plants. And remember that even the traditional vegetable plot can be designed and shaped so as to make an attractive feature.

As for fruit, you can grow a varied selection in the smallest of gardens simply by training trees against walls and fences. Where there is slightly more space at your disposal, a separate fruit garden would be feasible if you were to use the dwarf bushes now available (see Chapter 8).

6 Choosing a style

The character you choose to give your garden is really a matter of personal preference. And, generally, as long as it is applied with con-viction – rather than including a half-hearted mish-mash of styles – the result should be successful. The possibilities are endless, though,

FAMILY GARDEN

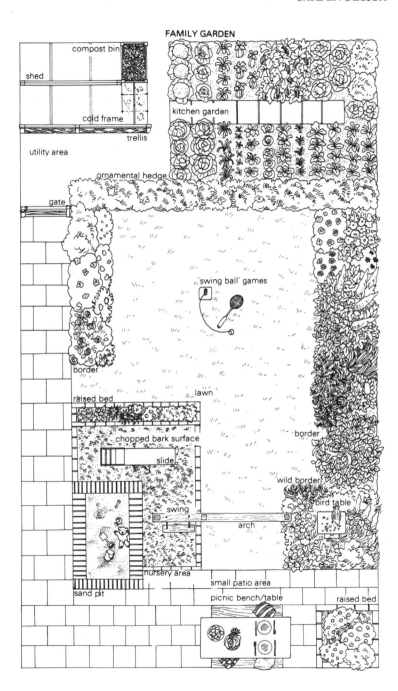

compost bin

shed

cold frame

trellis

utility area

kitchen garden

ornamental hedge

gate

swing ball' games

border

lawn

raised bed

chopped bark surface

border

slide

wild border

swing

bird table

arch

nursery area

small patio area

sand pit

picnic bench/table

raised bed

and so it might help to use the following as a starting point:

Houses with modern architecture: Keep the design bold and simple, using contemporary materials such as smooth paving, matching brickwork (if appropriate) and perhaps even gleaming timber. Plants, too, can be bold and sculptural. Avoid over-fussy detail and classical-style features.

Older and 'period' properties: Here a softer approach is generally more successful, using gentle contours, subtle plantings and more weathered-looking materials – rustic timber, for example, or textured stone. Details can be fairly ornate, but make sure that any items such as ornaments or archways are in keeping with the period of the house. Above all, avoid everything 'twee'!

7 Shaping up

The style you wish to adopt for your garden is the key factor when deciding how the various components should be shaped – whether the lawn, say, should have generous curves (for an informal look) or straight, precise edges (in the formal garden). Similarly, a patio or path could be set on the diagonal with a highly pronounced, staggering edge (for a contemporary feel) or be softly contoured with edges of cobbles mingling with plants (in a cottage-type garden).

Careful and appropriate shaping and placing of the individual elements is essential if your garden is to be an overall success. In effect, you are aiming to create a structural backbone to provide the all-important link between the many other features, and plants, that will eventually be included. So, rather than doing the job piecemeal, draw up a proper plan (see 'Planning on Paper', page 18).

8 Placing of permanent features

You can't afford to make mistakes when it comes to positioning permanent features like a lawn, patio or path – even fencing. You want to get it right first time and, to that end, you should once again plan on paper first. There are various factors that might affect the siting of these elements. Consider the following:

Lawns: Ideally, a lawn should receive plenty of light. Any areas of the garden that are heavily shaded – by overhanging trees or a building – might be better surfaced with paving materials or designated for borders. In the family garden you'll need to create a generous expanse of lawn for children's games and so forth. Finally, and this will sound rather obvious, bear in mind that lawns have to be cut – make sure that any areas laid to grass can be reached easily by a mower!

Patios: The conventional position for a patio is adjacent to the house,

LEISURE GARDEN

trellis

herb garden

fruit garden

seat

trellis

patio

stepping stones

border

lawn

pool

border

patio

bench

barbecue unit

garden furniture

pergola

tub

tub

bench

border

which makes sense because in summer it becomes a natural extension – an outdoor living room. For most people, patios also need to be reasonably sunny and sheltered. If the area immediately behind your house is in shade for the best part of the day, break with tradition and build your patio in a sunnier part of the garden – even bang in the middle if necessary. In big gardens it might be worth having more than one patio area, each positioned so that it catches the sun at a particular time of day. If too much sun is a problem, remember that shade can be provided with a pergola (a timber structure with overhead beams that can support climbing plants).

Paths: In theory, there are two sorts of path. One is totally practical, leading you to particular points in the garden (the shed or vegetable plot) by the most direct route. It will be wide enough to take machinery and equipment and the surface will be smooth and solid. The other is purely ornamental, designed to enhance the character of your garden and taking a route that will highlight special features and focal points along the way.

In practice, few gardens can accommodate both and so it's usually necessary to compromise somewhere between the two. Here are a few guidelines:

- In long, narrow gardens, a path that crosses it at an angle will make it appear wider – consider an S-shape;
- In short, wide gardens, go for a D-shaped or circular path as it will draw attention away from the sides towards the central area;
- In small gardens, avoid a straight, central path as it will cut the garden in two and make it look even smaller – any of the above options would be suitable, as would a straight path up one side of the garden.

Borders: By keeping borders to the perimeter of the garden you can create an enclosed environment where the boundaries are eventually all but completely camouflaged and the attention is held within the garden. This is especially effective in very small gardens. Where more space is available, you can also allow borders to form divisions within the garden – that way the whole garden isn't seen at a glance and you can create a few surprises around a corner or curve.

The most appropriate position for borders will also depend on the requirements of the plants you might wish to grow. Of course, no garden can provide ideal conditions for every plant in the book and so it will be necessary to compromise – the best plan is to site your borders so that they look visually pleasing (obviously taking full advantage of any sunny, sheltered areas) and then finding plants to suit (see tip number 9).

9 Planning for plants

The creation of a garden is a long-term affair. It takes time to establish plants and, in turn, to see the character of the garden develop and mature. The most common mistake in the new garden is to fill it with instant (yet only temporary) colour – all out of pots from the local garden centre and very costly! It might last the summer but, come autumn, the garden is as bare and bleak as ever.

A far better plan is to add plants to your garden layer by layer, starting with those that will provide a permanent backcloth of interest – just like an artist painting a picture. The sooner such plants are installed, the sooner the framework of the garden will be established.

The table below outlines the types of plants that will give the desired effect for each 'layer' of planting. For more detailed advice regarding the choice of plants, refer to the chapters indicated.

Effect	Types of plants	Comments
Permanent background	Evergreen shrubs, small trees and climbing plants (for walls/fences	Allow sufficient space to develop fully – see Chapter 5
Seasonal interest	Autumn- and winter-flowering/berrying shrubs; hardy perennials; bulbs	Permanent plantings for interest year-in, year-out – see Chapters 5 and 6
Fill-in colour and detail	Low-growing shrubs/perennials; annuals, biennials and bulbs	Ring the changes from year to year among permanent plants – see Chapters 5 and 6
Focal points and 'high spots'	Striking, specimen trees and shrubs with special form/colour; mass plantings of a single, favourite species of plant	Can be used within borders or isolated in lawn or on patio – see Chapters 5 and 9

10 Order of work

However eager, or desperate, you might be to get the work done, it doesn't pay to rush straight into a particular job. Planning ahead is the key to creating a successful garden design, and to ensure the whole project runs smoothly you should establish the order of work, taking into account:

- The time of year – certain jobs are best carried out at particular times (for example, ground preparation, turfing/sowing a lawn, planting);
- Your budget – you may have to spread the cost over a couple of years or more (see 'Spreading the Cost' page 20);

🖝 Your priorities – for some, a patio might be top of the list; for others, it might be a kitchen garden or a sandpit for the kids.
In principle, the main order of work should run as follows:
1 Clearing/preparing the site.
2 Planning on paper.
3 Establishing permanent features (lawn, patio and so on).
4 Preparing borders.
5 Planting permanent background plants.
6 Adding detail planting, ornamental features.

Planning on Paper

Drawing a scaled plan of your garden means you can experiment with design ideas to your heart's content, work out the best position for particular features and see what will or won't fit in – all in the comfort of your living room. It is always worth spending some time in planning the garden on paper before you invest time and money on ideas which may not, in practice, work out very well in the available space. And don't worry about the plan being a work of art – far more important is that the scale/dimensions are accurate and that you, at least, understand it.

Measuring up
First establish the exact dimensions and shape of your garden in relation to the house and also the position of any existing features such as a tree or shed. To this end you will have to get out into the garden armed with a notepad and pencil, measuring tape or steel rule, a bunch of short wooden sticks or tent pegs and a reel of string. The procedure, then, is as follows:
1 Start at the house, marking a fixed point at each corner (A and B) or, in a terraced house, at each boundary. Measure the width of the house, taking into account any protrusions and so on, and note it down.
2 From point A, measure to the furthest point of the garden on the left (C). Now measure from B to C, writing down each measurement as you go along and making sketches if necessary. Repeat the process on the right-hand side of the garden, measuring from A to D and B to D.
3 Use this method of triangulation (see diagram) to measure between other fixed points in the garden and then transfer them to your drawing, noting them all down so that you can later establish the exact position of side boundaries, trees etc.

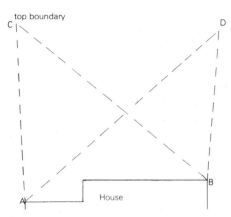

Drawing the plan

The principle involved in the creation of a scale plan from your various measurements is the same as that of a dot-to-dot drawing. You have to mark down the exact position of all the fixed points so that you can draw from one to the other to form an accurate outline of your garden.

To transfer the measurements to paper you follow exactly the same procedure as you did in the garden except this time you need to be armed with a large compass (or piece of string attached to a pencil – see diagram), ruler and graph paper. And you need to choose an appropriate scale to which you can translate your measurements.

As a rough guide, an A3 size (420 × 297 mm) sheet of graph paper, using a scale where 20 mm represents 1 m, would accommodate a garden measuring up to 21 × 15 m (69 × 49 ft). Where more space is needed, you can stick two sheets of paper together, or if the garden is much smaller you can increase the scale.

Now you can get down to business:

1 Start by drawing in the outline of the house and marking the A and B positions.

2 Refer to your first measurement (A to C) and translate it into your chosen scale.

3 Set the compass to the correct span by measuring against a ruler.

4 With the point of the compass at A, draw an arc in the top left-hand corner.

5 Repeat the process with the second measurement (B to C), drawing an arc with the compass point at B.

6 The point where the two arcs cross is your C marker.

7 Continue in the same way with each set of measurements until the plan is complete.

Adding the detail

Once you have drawn in the outline of your garden and positioned any existing features, it's a good idea to keep it as a 'master plan' by drawing on tracing paper placed over the top. This way you can experiment with your various ideas without any danger of endless rubbings-out ruining the original.

Remember that all the features you include must be drawn to the same scale. And try to include as much detail as possible so that the plan serves as a constant pictorial reminder of the sort of effect you are creating.

Spreading the Cost

There's no getting away from the fact that gardens can prove costly, both to create and maintain. A single, sizeable shrub from the local nursery or garden centre is going to have a price tag of at least £4–5; a decent lawnmower will have one of at least £50. But don't panic! Your budget might be limited but that doesn't mean you have to wave goodbye to the garden of your dreams.

The secret, once again, lies in forward planning – plus, perhaps, a touch of trickery and an eye for a bargain (we'll come to that later). First, you should work out how much you can afford to spend right away. Then decide how the money would be best allocated, bearing in mind the following points:

- Don't attempt to create an instant garden as it will invariably mean doing it 'on the cheap';
- Rather than concentrating on just one or two special features, consider every aspect of the garden and spend some money on each;
- Do the work yourself – it will be considerably cheaper than employing a local landscape contractor. However, be realistic and plan only features that are within your capabilities;
- When buying plants, materials and equipment, always shop around to make sure you get the best deal.

Saving ways

Lawns: Sowing grass seed is always a lot cheaper than turfing (see Chapter 4).

Hard surfaces: Concrete costs the least and can be given an attractive finish by exposing the aggregate or by colouring it with a concrete dye. At a later date it could always be topped with paving stones. A combination of paving slabs and gravel is another relatively cheap option.

Boundaries: Consider using cheap wire fencing (you can camouflage it with quick-growing climbers) until you can afford to replace it with something more ornamental or substantial.

Plants: Ideally, spend the bulk of the money initially allocated on just a few sizeable, well-placed shrubs, chosen to provide year-round interest and to form that all-important permanent backcloth. But there may be more urgent priorities, of course, such as creating an effective windbreak.

You'll certainly be quids in if you raise your own plants from seed (see Chapter 3) and use these to provide colour and interest around the bought-in shrubs. Other 'specimen' plants can be added as and when the money allows.

Always buy from reputable nurseries, though, rather than take a risk with so-called bargains from the back of a van in a market. However, there's no harm in getting something for nothing from friends' and neighbours' gardens – just make sure you ask first! – and you can often find some real gems, costing a matter of pence, on the plant stalls at local fêtes and other events.

Tools and equipment: It's quality not quantity that is the all-important factor here. Forget the fancy gadgets and go all out for the best garden fork, spade and rake your money can buy. They should last you a lifetime – cheap ones will last you a season.

Most other items of equipment can be bought as and when needed – come early summer, for example, a lawnmower, hose and sprinkler will probably be top priorities. Bear in mind, too, that for one-off or less frequent jobs (such as ground clearance or hedge-trimming) there are hire shops that rent out the necessary equipment at very reasonable rates.

CHAPTER 2

SOIL

The ground under our feet should be suffering from one enormous inferiority complex. People marvel at wonderful landscapes, parks and gardens, and treasure the trees in their towns and cities, but rarely pay the slightest attention to the one all-important, life-giving ingredient – soil. Until, that is, they have a garden of their own. All of a sudden, that 'boring brown stuff' has to be tended and planted and put to work.

Whether left to its own devices or cultivated in fields and gardens, soil supports an amazing range of plant life. However, there's no universal soil standard and its make-up can vary considerably from area to area – even from one end of a road to the other. In the absence of any human interference, land will be colonised only by those plants that appreciate the soil conditions. But that's no use to gardeners, of course – we want to grow what we like!

As you will see, each soil type has very different characteristics, some of which are far more desirable than others when it comes to growing a full and healthy range of garden plants. But that doesn't mean you necessarily have to accept the status quo. A great deal can be done to improve your soil and make it as near-ideal as possible.

What to Aim For

It's the nature and quality of the top layer of earth, or topsoil, in your garden that most affects the well-being of plants. It should extend over the whole plot to a depth of 23 cm (9 in) or so and, compared to the subsoil underneath, should be quite dark and crumbly. These two qualities, in fact, are the key characteristics of a good garden soil because both indicate the presence of humus – a 'living' organic substance that results from decayed vegetable and animal matter being broken down by bacteria, worms and the like. It is this humus that provides a home for millions of friendly soil organisms and food for the plants, holds moisture and gives the soil a good, friable texture. It's the stuff of life in all soils, but they all vary considerably, depending on their content of clay, sand and chalk. Most soils contain a little of each. The very best soil is called 'medium loam' and it really is a

UNEVEN GROUND

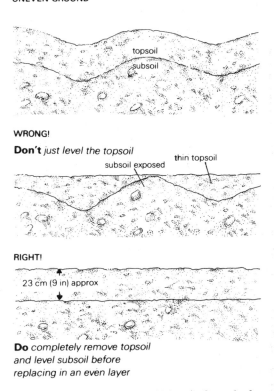

topsoil
subsoil

WRONG!

Don't *just level the topsoil*

subsoil exposed   thin topsoil

RIGHT!

23 cm (9 in) approx

Do *completely remove topsoil
and level subsoil before
replacing in an even layer*

gardener's dream because it is an ideal blend of sand, clay and chalk. Its texture is neither too heavy nor too light, it holds water without becoming waterlogged, and its chemical make-up is neither too acid nor too limy (see the table on page 24). All these factors allow the humus and its resident colony of organisms to work effectively and that, in turn, means the plants are kept happy and the gardener has less work to do!

The table will help you to identify the type of soil you have in your garden. Most soils, of course, are a mixture of some or all of the constituents described. If you don't happen to hold the trump card of a medium loam, don't despair – few of us do! The suggested improvements and a little long-term pampering can work wonders on the worst of soils. It should be noted, though, that if builders have left a particularly poor, thin or uneven layer of topsoil in the garden, it may be a good idea to buy in a fresh supply rather than battle on with what you have.

WHAT TYPE OF SOIL DO YOU HAVE?			
What is it like?	Soil type	Pros and cons	Improvements
Red–brown and smooth; usually wet-looking in solid clods	Clay	Fairly high humus content but holds a lot of water – beneficial in dry spells. Heavy and cold – plants late to start growing	Double-dig in autumn to let frost break it down. Improve texture/drainage with coarse grit and add organic matter every year. If necessary, add lime to reduce acidity. Keep off it in wet weather
Very dark brown and spongy to the touch	Peat	Quite good texture and high humus content but acidity stops it working	Make it more alkaline by adding lime and so improve fertility
Light in colour, perhaps yellowish, with dry, fine particles; gritty to touch	Sand	Easy to work and free-draining. Also warms up for early growth. Low humus	Improve water retention/fertility by adding organic and plant food material every year
Thin soil, darker on top but very light underneath with whitish particles	Chalk	Little humus and difficult to work. Sticky when wet but quick to dry	Buy in fresh topsoil if in very poor condition. Add organic matter every year to improve structure and fertility

Acid or Alkaline?

If you live in an area where the underlying rock is chalk or limestone, it's fairly likely that your soil will be at least slightly alkaline. If, on the other hand, your garden sits on top of granite, the soil will tend to be more acid. Certainly, that's the theory, although in practice it's not unknown to have pockets of acid soil and alkaline soil all in the one garden.

The vast majority of plants are relatively tolerant but do best when the soil is fairly neutral – not very acid or alkaline. For some, however, an acid soil is imperative (rhododendrons, azaleas, some heathers, for example) and for others a high lime (alkaline) content is the order of the day (the cabbage family is one of these).

Knowing the level of acidity or alkalinity in your garden soil will mean you can either steer clear of those plants that don't like the conditions you have, or you can try to make the soil more neutral. However, while it's fairly easy to make an acid soil more alkaline (by adding lime), it's virtually impossible to make an alkaline soil more acid. You can buy specially prepared acid (or ericaceous) soil from garden centres, though, which means even people with an alkaline soil can grow rhododendrons and the like if they confine them to containers or specially created raised beds.

The level of acidity/alkalinity is measured on a numeric scale called pH. The higher the number, the more limy the soil, the lower the number, the more acid. Garden soil generally ranges from pH4 to pH8.5, with the neutral and most desirable value being pH6.5 or pH7. You can buy special soil-testing kits very cheaply from garden centres and they are dead easy to use.

How Digging Helps

For every gardener who claims digging is therapeutic, there must be a hundred others who find it a pain in the neck, or back! The good news, however, is that in the ornamental garden the earth needs really thorough digging only when new borders are being created or when the ground is being prepared for sowing or turfing a lawn. And that may be only once in the lifetime of the garden. It's usual for the vegetable plot to be dug over each year, prior to sowing or planting, although if the ground is really well prepared initially, this subsequent digging isn't likely to be particularly arduous. In any event, digging is best carried out when ground conditions are favourable, usually in early spring for light soil and autumn if it's heavy.

Digging helps to improve the ground, and in turn benefits your plants, in two ways. First, it breaks up the soil and creates a healthier texture by letting air in so that it can 'breathe'. Second, it provides a convenient opportunity to get an extra supply of plant food and good organic matter into the earth – say, in the form of well-rotted manure or home-made compost.

There is single-digging, which means the soil is dug to the depth of a spade (around 23 cm/9 in – often referred to as a 'spit'), and there is double-digging, which is rather more complicated and involves going twice as deep. For most purposes, single-digging is perfectly adequate. On heavy clay soils, and especially in brand-new gardens, however, double-digging, with the addition of plenty of organic matter, will improve the texture of the soil making it more free-draining.

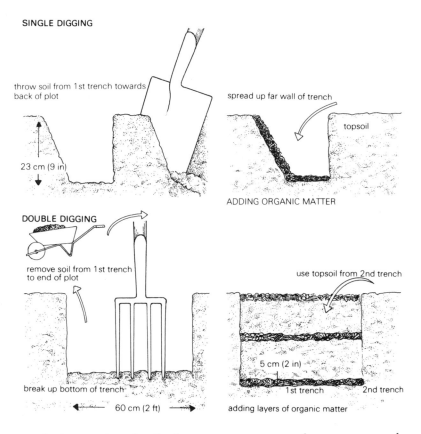

SINGLE DIGGING

throw soil from 1st trench towards back of plot

spread up far wall of trench

topsoil

23 cm (9 in)

ADDING ORGANIC MATTER

DOUBLE DIGGING

remove soil from 1st trench to end of plot

use topsoil from 2nd trench

5 cm (2 in)

break up bottom of trench

60 cm (2 ft)

1st trench   2nd trench

adding layers of organic matter

Single-digging: Start by digging out a narrow trench across one end of the plot, to the depth of a spade. As you remove the earth, just throw it straight behind you as far as you can. Put a good 5 cm (2 in) layer of manure, garden compost or spent mushroom compost in the trench and then start digging another one immediately behind it, using the earth you remove from this to fill the first trench. When you add the organic matter, put it up the far wall of the trench to make sure that it's mixed right through the topsoil and not just in the bottom few inches.

Double-digging: Here you dig a 60 cm (2 ft) wide trench and remove the soil to the end of the plot to be used in refilling the last trench. Then break up the bottom with a fork, put in a 5 cm (2 in) layer of organic matter and half fill with earth. Add another layer of organic matter and completely fill the trench with a final layer of manure or compost.

Feeding the Soil

A ready supply of food is vital if plants are to flourish. And since it is soil organisms that release many of the minerals and nutrients essential to healthy growth, the main task is to build up as high a humus content in the soil as possible. Not that this is a one-off job: however good your soil is in the first place, the humus content won't be sufficient to sustain your plants indefinitely; nor will the humus necessarily supply enough of the most important minerals. That's why it needs a helping hand in the form of regular applications of manures and fertilisers.

The easiest way to define these two forms of plant food is to categorise them as manures which are bulky and fertilisers which are either granulated, powdered or in liquid form and come out of a bag or bottle.

Manures: Top of the list in this category is well-rotted farmyard manure, closely followed by home-made garden compost (see page 28). These can be applied to the soil as a matter of routine once a year, and also as part of ground preparation for planting roses, shrubs, fruit and so on. However, as it will probably take a good year for your new compost heap to 'bear fruit' and farmyard manure isn't that readily available, you may have to get your soil off to a good start with bought-in mushroom compost or, as a last resort, peat. Peat is quite expensive, while garden compost comes virtually free. Other good organic manures include spent hops and rotted seaweed.

Fertilisers: The reason we sometimes have to use this type of plant food in addition to organic types is that the latter won't always supply sufficient quantities of three essential minerals – namely, nitrogen (N), phosphorus (P) and potash (K). A balanced fertiliser will contain equal proportions of all three.

HOW INORGANIC FERTILISERS HELP		
Mineral	**What it does**	**Signs of deficiency**
Nitrogen	Encourages strong and healthy leaves and stems	Sparse foliage, pale leaf colour, spindly stems
Phosphorus	Encourages good root development	Slow growth – on inspection root system small and weak
Potash	Encourages flowers and fruit	No obvious signs – light soils usually deficient

However, because some plants prefer, say, higher nitrogen or potash levels than others – and since each mineral has a different effect
on plant growth – there's also a whole range of fertilisers where the
proportions (N:P:K ratio) have been formulated for specific plants
or for special purposes. Fertilisers come in granule, powder or liquid
form and all are clearly labelled as to the job they will do and how
often they should be applied. But the latter is a crucial factor – unlike
most humans, plants are slow to recover from over-indulgence!

Generally you'll need only three bags of fertiliser: rose fertiliser for
all flowers and fruit, Growmore for vegetables and bonemeal when
you're planting. If you're organically minded, blood, fish and bonemeal will do most jobs.

On the Compost Heap

If you can spare just a few square feet of your garden to make room
for a compost bin, you'll have a constant supply of highly nutritious
organic matter that will cost you hardly a bean. And with conserva-
tion so much on our minds these days, you can also feel fairly pleased
with yourself over the years that virtually none of your kitchen scraps
or plant debris is having to be carted away by the binmen in so many
polythene sacks!

When building a compost heap, the aim is to create an environment where bacteria will thrive and, in turn, break down the vegetable contents into a reasonably pleasant-to-handle, dark, crumbly
matter – much the same as peat. To this end, it's important to get the
right balance of material in the bin and to maintain the sort of conditions that will allow the bacteria to complete the job properly.

The right type of bin
If your compost heap can be screened or hidden from view, there's
really no need to worry about trying to make it look pretty. And that
means you can go for a traditional, wooden bin, which is quite easy to
make yourself. There are plenty of plastic jobs available at garden
centres too. If you've got the space, it's a good idea to have two bins
side by side so that one can be 'maturing' and ready to use while the
second is still being prepared.

There are various rather more sophisticated models available in
the shops (at a price), but while they might look more attractive
there's no guarantee that they'll necessarily produce better compost.
The most important things to look for in a bin are:

- A good size – if it's too small there won't be sufficient weight/volume of material inside for the composting process to work. A 1 m (3 ft) cube, or equivalent capacity, is the ideal;
- Air holes for ventilation underneath but not in the sides;
- Durable, solid construction – wooden bins will need to be treated with a good preservative. Plastic types can be very hard-wearing;
- Convenient access, both for inserting material and removing compost at base.

THE MAIN INGREDIENTS		
	What to put in	**What to leave out**
From the garden	Annual weeds, grass cuttings, leafy clippings, rotting leaves, dead flowers, crop remains, fresh manure, straw	Perennial/persistent weeds, soil (shake off roots), any material that's been treated with weedkiller or is diseased, woody stems
From the house	Fresh vegetable scraps, tea leaves, coffee grounds, egg shells, fruit and vegetable peelings	Meat, fish and bread (will attract vermin, etc.), plastic or metal packaging material, newspaper, fire ashes

Building the heap
- Start with a layer of coarse material that allows air to get in at the bottom.
- Grass cuttings should be mixed in with other material to let some air into them. Similarly, any compacted bundles of garden waste should be shaken loose.
- Add as wide a variety of ingredients as possible in shallow layers, wetting very dry material first.
- Keep the heap covered to retain heat.
- Turn the compost a couple of times by throwing it out of the bin and then throwing it back again. This sounds like a lot of work but it makes all the difference.

Using the compost
A well-made heap should be starting to supply you with usable garden compost within three to six months, depending on whether it has been made during summer or winter. The more protection you can give it during the colder, wetter months, the better. To give your soil a treat, spread a liberal quantity over the ground in autumn and use it on a regular basis when preparing planting sites.

CHAPTER 3

PLANTS FROM SEED

Even if money were no object, it would be a terrible shame to buy in all the plants you want to include in your garden. For apart from saving you a small fortune over the years, raising ornamentals and vegetables yourself from seed allows you to grow a far wider range of varieties, to get more plants for your money, to make sure they have the best possible start in life and, perhaps most important of all, to have the satisfaction of saying, 'I grew that!'

There are two common misconceptions regarding this method of plant raising: one is that it involves a host of sophisticated equipment and complicated techniques; the other is that you need do little more than scatter the seed on a bare patch of ground! The truth, in fact, lies somewhere in between. You certainly don't need to have a greenhouse but you do have to provide a little tender, loving care.

It pays enormous dividends to do your homework first and find out as much as possible about the various plants you want to grow. Apart from gardening books and magazines, an invaluable source of information is the catalogues from the major seed firms. If you send off for them well in advance of the main sowing season, which starts in March/April, you can leaf through them at leisure and do your planning and ordering in plenty of time. It will also allow you to organise your sowing schedule so that you have plants doing what you want them to do at the right time of year!

Incidentally, many seed firms offer attractive incentives for early ordering – for example, before the end of November. This would be no bad idea, especially in the future, as it means you are planning for the following year when the past season's successes and failures (and we all have them!) are still fresh in your mind.

To Sow Outside or Under Cover?

You can raise a huge range of plants for summer colour simply by sowing directly into the ground, in the exact position you want the plants to grow. The same goes for vegetables, although here the timing of the sowings will vary considerably according to the crop and when you want to pick it (see Chapter 7). There are occasions, however, when it is beneficial to sow seed into seedtrays or pots of compost so that the young plants can be started off protected under cover – either on the windowsill, say, or in a coldframe (a sort of mini-greenhouse).

This method is most often used in order to produce young plants that much earlier in the season – so that they are ready to be planted out when you would otherwise still be sowing – and to raise tender plants that cannot be sown outside until all danger of cold and frost has passed.

Seed for the Flower Border

The plants you grow from seed in the flower border are divided according to their essential requirements and growing behaviour into three main categories, each of which demands slightly different sowing procedures and aftercare.

Annuals: There are hardy annuals (denoted HA in seed catalogues) and half-hardy annuals (HHA), all of which are sown to provide flowers or foliage interest in the same year, after which the plant dies – usually by late autumn. They are then dug up and thrown away (ideally, on to the compost heap so that they can benefit your garden even in after-life!). Hardy annuals are tough characters and both the seed and seedling plants will survive a bit of late frost, which means they can be sown outside quite early on. Examples are pot marigolds and candytuft. Half-hardy annuals are more tender and, while they will put up with quite cold conditions, they won't tolerate the slightest frosting – that generally means starting them off under cover. Examples are French marigolds and petunias.

Biennials: The plants in this category are so named because, from a summer sowing outside, they will produce foliage in the first year and flowers in the next. When flowering is finished, the plants will eventually die, like annuals, and they should then be removed from the flower border. Examples are wallflowers, sweet Williams and foxgloves.

Perennials: Unlike annuals and biennials, these don't die – some might appear to die off in winter but they are only 'resting', coming back into growth when conditions are favourable. Many of them are very easy to grow from seed, needing no special equipment or know-how. If you're on a small budget, they're the cheapest and best way to fill the borders. Examples are lupins, delphiniums, phlox, chrysan-themums and polyanthus.

Sowing flowers outside

Careful planning is the key to a successful flower border, so try to resist the temptation of simply snapping up the seed packets that have the prettiest pictures. The most important pictures, in fact, should be in your head – one of the border as it is now, with all its strengths and weaknesses, and one of how the same border might look in six months' time. For the more accurately you can visualise the effect you want to create, the better chance you will have of choosing the right plants for the job. It will also make life a whole lot easier when it comes to planning what to sow where.

First it's important to ascertain the plants' basic requirements in terms of position (sun/shade) and soil requirements (acid/normal/alkaline). Then consider the following:

- Flowering period – to avoid having prominent 'dead areas', position plants so that there will be some colour and interest throughout the border at any given time;
- Flower colour – ideally, you will have a specific colour scheme in mind when choosing which plants to grow. In any event, avoid any unfortunate clashes by taking into account the flower colour of adjacent plants. (Sticking to colours that are natural neighbours in the colour spectrum is usually the safest bet – for example, yellow next to orange next to scarlet, or pink next to purple next to blue);
- Plant size – always double-check the ultimate height of a particular group of plants so that you know whether it should be placed towards the back or front of the border for best effect. And make sure you follow the instructions on the seed packet relating to spacing – otherwise the plants might be either too sparse or too cramped.

Sowing hardy annuals

While the information on the seed packet will include a recommended sowing period, the ideal time for sowing hardy annuals will be governed by the weather and the ground conditions. Generally March to early April is ideal, though whatever type of seed you are sowing, the ground must be neither frozen nor waterlogged. It is to be hoped that you will have had a chance to dig over the ground in the previous autumn, incorporating some good organic matter to help sustain your plants. To this end, it's also a good idea to apply a light dressing of rose fertiliser just a couple of weeks before you plan to sow. Then, just as soon as the time is right, you can proceed as follows:

SOWING HARDY ANNUALS

1 Use stick to mark out areas to be sown

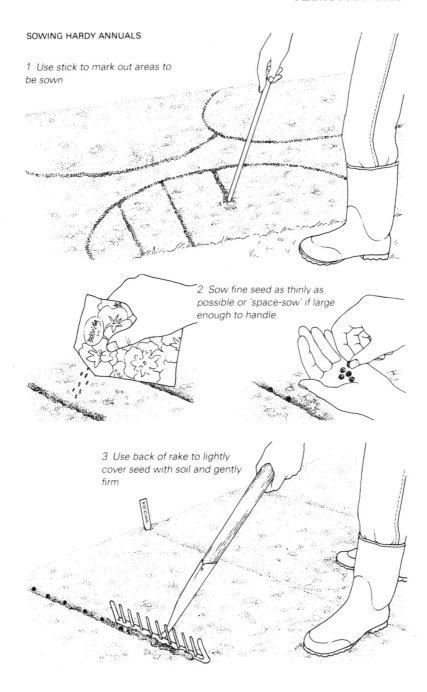

2 Sow fine seed as thinly as possible or 'space-sow' if large enough to handle

3 Use back of rake to lightly cover seed with soil and gently firm

1 Rake over the ground to be sown, getting rid of all the lumps and bumps and any large stones and so on, to leave a level, crumbly surface.

2 Using a stick to draw lines in the soil, mark out the areas you want the various plants to occupy – this is the creative bit! As a general rule, give each group of plants sufficient space to make a real impact. And rather than having them in uniform blocks, try to arrange the individual areas so that they meander and curve, perhaps wrapping around one another. That way you'll have a more natural intermingling of plants, with one group drifting into the next.

3 The above process will probably have forced you to make a final decision as to which plants are going to occupy a given area. In any event, double-check that you know exactly what's going where, taking into account each plant's flowering period, flower colour and plant size.

4 Still using a stick, draw furrows within the outlined areas, to the seed-sowing depth indicated on the seed packet. This is usually fairly shallow for annuals – don't be tempted to sow any deeper. The furrows, or drills, should be spaced about 15–23 cm (6–9 in) apart but, again, be guided by the instructions. Drills are best made in straight, parallel lines so that you'll have no trouble later on distinguishing the seedlings from common garden weeds!

5 Sow the seeds in the drills, spacing them as recommended on the seed packet and taking particular care with fine seed – try to sprinkle this along the drill as evenly and thinly as possible.

6 Gently cover the seed with soil from along the edge of the drill using the lightest touch of a rake. Label each area of plants.

7 The whole area can then be slightly firmed down with the back of the rake.

8 Keep an eye open for any neighbourhood cats that might be attracted to your freshly prepared ground and take appropriate action if necessary – a network of cotton between sticks might deter them. If the weather stays dry, water to keep the ground just moist, using a fine rose fitted to the watering can.

9 Once the young seedlings are big enough to handle fairly easily, remove the weakest to leave strong ones growing at the recommended distance apart – again, be guided by what it says on the seed packet.

10 A further thinning of the plants may be necessary later on – don't be tempted to hang on to more plants than is recommended (or looks right) as both the plants and the overall display will suffer in the long run.

THINNING OUT

*Remove weakest seedlings to
leave strong ones growing at
the recommended distance*

Sowing perennials and biennials

Perennials and biennials are sown outside in shallow drills in May/
June. When they are big enough to handle comfortably, transplant
them about 15 cm (6 in) apart. Move them to their permanent position in the border in autumn or in spring of the following year.

Seed for the Vegetable Plot

The timing of sowings in the kitchen garden varies considerably
because it is governed by the individual crop's natural growing season and how long each takes to reach maturity and be ready for picking (refer to Chapter 7 for specific details in this respect). Through
careful selection and planning, therefore, it's possible for your plot to
be earning its keep all year round and for you to have one or more of
your favourite vegetables ripe for the table at any given time. And
while this can be achieved with outside sowings only, you'll find you
can enjoy an even wider variety of crops – and be eating many of
them when they're yet to reach the greengrocers' shelves – if you are
also prepared to start a few off under cover.

Choosing which vegetables to grow and planning for year-round
cropping is, again, something to do in the winter, using the seed catalogues. If space is limited, choose first those vegetables that taste
much better really fresh – sweetcorn, spinach and all the salads.

Sowing vegetables outside

Ground preparation for vegetables is the same as for ornamentals,
although you should try to make a particularly good job of the
autumn digging, incorporating plenty of organic matter, if you want
the crops to be especially healthy and tasty.

The seed sowing procedure is the same, too, except that in the vegetable plot you will be creating drills in straight parallel lines across the plot, with anything from 15–45 cm (6–18 in) between the rows, depending on the spacing requirements of the individual crops. Once they're through, the young seedlings will need to be thinned out according to the instructions on the seed packet. This is just a case of carefully pulling out the excess, leaving plants at the recommended spacings. Sometimes the excess seedlings can be transplanted – again, the seed packet or catalogue will guide you as to spacing. When transplanting, proceed as follows:

1 Prepare the final planting positions, spaced as recommended, before lifting the seedlings. Then try to work quickly but diligently.

2 Lift each of the seedlings in turn, using a trowel to dig around the root system and ease it out of the ground while gently supporting the young leaves/stem.

3 Make sure that the planting holes will comfortably accommodate the root system but never plant the seedlings any deeper than they were in the seedbed (check that the soil mark on the stem is level with the surface).

TRANSPLANTING

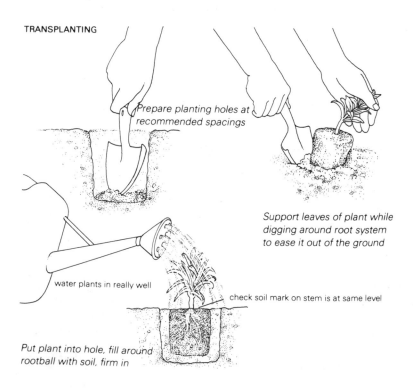

Prepare planting holes at recommended spacings

Support leaves of plant while digging around root system to ease it out of the ground

water plants in really well

check soil mark on stem is at same level

Put plant into hole, fill around rootball with soil, firm in

4 Fill in around the roots with soil and firm down, again checking the soil level against the stems. Generously water the plants in.

Vegetables to sow and grow in situ: Beans – French, broad, runner; beetroot; carrot; cucumber; courgette; endive; fennel; lettuce; onion; parsnip; peas; radish; spinach; tomato (outdoor); turnip.

Vegetables to sow and transplant: Broccoli; Brussels sprout; cabbage; cauliflower; kale; leek; lettuce.

MAKE SENSE OF THE SEED TERMS	
Chitted	The seed is pre-germinated by the supplier and so must be planted immediately it is received
Dressed	The seed has been coated with a fungicide and/or pesticide prior to being packaged
F1	These seeds have more vigour, uniformity and resistance to disease. They are always more expensive
Pelleted	The seed has a special, thickish coating to make it easier to handle – useful with finer seeds
Damping off	Seedlings suddenly collapse and die – main cause is wet/humid conditions and overcrowding
True leaves	The plant's first proper leaves – not the seed leaves that appear immediately after germination

Sowing Under Cover

As outlined previously, if you want to grow a few of the more tender garden plants or give ornamentals and vegetables an earlier start than outside sowing would allow, you will have to provide the seeds with some protection from the elements. When this method of seed raising is recommended on seed packets, for whatever reason, the most usual instruction is to sow 'under glass'. And while this might be self-explanatory to more experienced gardeners, it leaves a host of first-timers with the mistaken impression that the seed has to be sown in a greenhouse and they promptly put the packet back on the rack!

The truth, in fact, is that such seeds will germinate perfectly well on a bright, reasonably warm windowsill, perhaps in the kitchen or a spare bedroom. If you haven't got any windowsills, you could consider rigging up some temporary shelving across the window – after all, the seeds will probably need to be there for only a matter of weeks. An alternative would be to find room in the garden for a coldframe, which is a low box-like structure, usually made from wood, with a slightly sloping, hinged glass roof (if you make your own, you could use an old window). As long as the coldframe is in a fairly light, sunny position, it will provide sufficient protection from frost to raise all but the most tender of plants just that bit earlier in the year. Over the years, it will also prove enormously useful when you want to, say, increase your stock of garden plants by taking cuttings or perhaps overwinter dahlia tubers and so forth.

While a coldframe can be made or bought for a fairly reasonable price (especially compared to a greenhouse), you may think it an undue expense if you're going to be raising only a few plants. Or you may simply not be able to spare the necessary few square feet in your garden. The solution here – and also if you've ruled out windowsill sowing – is to sow outside in open ground but with the protection of cloches. This method, as explained later on, can be every bit as successful and will cost you just the price of the cloches which, being little more than polythene and wire, are extremely cheap.

When to start sowing
On the windowsill: Plan to start sowing seed from early March until late May.
In the coldframe: You can start plants off three to four weeks earlier than if they were sown outside. Protect from frost at night by covering the frame with sacking or an old piece of carpet.
Under cloches: By allowing the cloches to warm up the ground prior to sowing, you can usually get seeds started three to four weeks earlier than if unprotected.

Sowing in containers
If you're using a windowsill or coldframe, the seed will have to be sown in containers of specially prepared, bought-in compost. These are the two essentials but, as you will see from the table below, you will also need a few other items in order to do the job properly.

The best plan is to clear the draining board in the kitchen and use this, covered with newspaper, as your work bench. That way, you can have water to hand, both for watering and general mopping up, and you can surround yourself with all the necessary paraphernalia without unduly disturbing the rest of the family – just as long as Sunday lunch isn't on the go!

What you need	Special comments
Containers	Above all, these must be clean, have plenty of drainage holes and be large enough to take the quantity of seed you are sowing. For small quantities of seedlings, pots are generally big enough. For larger quantities use seedtrays
Compost	For most purposes, a pre-packed 'seed' compost should be used – not a 'potting' type. Use it as it comes and never mix it with garden soil
Sieve	To sift the compost used for covering the seed – the finer the compost, the better. Alternatively, break down the compost by rubbing it between your palms and sprinkle it over
Covering	Each seedtray will need to be covered with a piece of glass or clear plastic to help keep the seed moist and warm. For most seeds cling-film is ideal
Newspaper	A sheet of newspaper goes over the glass to exclude light and aid germination – check the seed packet instructions, though, as this isn't always needed

1 Fill the seedtray or pot right to the rim with compost.

2 Firm down, not over-heavily, to leave a nice, even surface.

3 Always water *before* sowing.

4 Pour some seed into the palm of your hand and use the fingers of the other hand to sprinkle it, little by little, in a fine layer over the compost. Larger seed can be individually spaced out over the surface.

5 If the seed is very fine, simply press it down into the compost with the bottom of another pot or a piece of wood. Don't cover very fine seed.

6 Larger seed will need to be covered with a fine layer of freshly sifted compost – make sure that it's spread evenly over the surface.

7 Label the seedtray, writing the name of the plant and the variety – even the flower colour if appropriate.

8 Cover the seedtray with a sheet of glass or clear plastic, followed by newspaper (if necessary), and place it on the allocated windowsill or in the coldframe. Keep the frame firmly closed and protect from frost at night. Some seeds need higher temperatures than others to germinate and these can be put in the airing cupboard – the top shelf is generally ideal. Look at them every day for the first signs of germination. An alternative is to invest in a small electric propagator which is pre-set to about the right temperature.

9 Keep a close eye on the trays and as soon as you see signs of germination – the tips of seedlings emerging – remove both the newspaper
and glass. Make sure that the trays now receive plenty of light, though
not direct sunlight.
10 Water just to keep the compost moist.

SOWING UNDER COVER

2 *Sprinkle fine seed evenly over
the surface (space-sow larger
seed)*

1 *Fill seed tray/pots to brim
with compost and gently firm
down before sowing*

Press in very fine seed
with a piece of wood

3 *Cover larger seeds with an even layer
of sifted compost*

Use the base of a pot for seed sown in pots

4 *Cover seed trays/pots with
sheet of glass or plastic or cling
film, followed by newspaper (if
required). Place on windowsill
or in coldframe/airing cupboard
as appropriate*

How to grow on

The following sequence of events is geared to producing healthy, strong-growing, young plants that will survive the shock of being moved to their final growing position outside as soon as conditions allow. As you will see, there's no set time for carrying out the various operations. In the main, therefore, you will have to be guided first by the state of the seedlings – their rate of growth and general well-being – and second by the state of the weather.

Pricking out: This is a wonderfully descriptive term for a process that will give the seedlings more space to grow. At the same time you can get rid of any that failed to germinate successfully or are looking particularly weak. The job should be done as soon as the seedlings are big enough to be handled comfortably. You will need:

🖝 A clean seedtray or some small pots;

🖝 A fresh supply of potting compost;

🖝 A dibber (special tool for making planting holes) or an old pencil.

PRICKING OUT SEEDLINGS

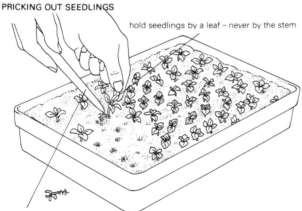

hold seedlings by a leaf – *never* by the stem

use dibber to tease out roots from compost

Prepare the fresh tray of compost the day before in the same way as for sowing. Use the dibber gently to loosen the earth around a few at a time. Then lift an individual seedling by holding on to a seed leaf (never the stem) and teasing the roots out of the compost with the stick. Still holding the seedling by a leaf, use the other hand to make a hole with the dibber in the fresh compost. Lower the roots into the hole and gently firm the compost around the stem. Continue in the same way until you have pricked out the required number of healthy seedlings – they should be fairly uniformly placed in the new tray, about 2.5 cm (1 in) or so apart. Water gently from above, using a fine spray, and place the tray on the windowsill or in the coldframe.

Hardening off: Plants that are being raised under cover need to be slowly acclimatised to the less favourable conditions they are going to encounter when finally moved outside with no protection at all. In effect, they need to be toughened up. Start hardening off about three to four weeks before planting outside.

If the tray has been on a warm windowsill, move it somewhere slightly cooler, but equally bright, for a week or so. Then, as soon as all danger of daytime frost has passed, find a spot outside for the tray, making sure that it is reasonably sheltered from rain and cold winds – this is where a coldframe is ideal. Bring them in at night until the weather warms up enough for them to stay out. This is normally late May to early June.

If the seedlings have been in a coldframe from the start, all you need to do is gradually increase the ventilation, opening the lights just a little at first – during the day only – and eventually removing them altogether as long as the weather is fine. Still protect from frost, though, if necessary. After about two weeks the plants can be left uncovered at night as well, and they can be transplanted as soon as ground conditions are suitable.

Transplanting: Check that the planting site is neither too wet nor too dry and that the soil is reasonably warm. If necessary, water both the seedlings and the ground the day before you are due to transplant. The method is exactly the same as described for transplanting seedling vegetables raised outside – just make sure that you stick to the planting distances recommended on the seed packet, which, it is to be hoped, you haven't thrown away! Incidentally, remember that half-used packets of seed can be saved for the following year as long as they're kept air-tight.

Sowing under cloches

The method for cloches is identical to sowing outside in drills, except that the cloches are placed over the prepared seedbed a good fortnight before sowing. Because the ground underneath is then protected from rain and chilling air, it soon warms up, which means seed can be sown that much earlier. As the weather improves, more ventilation can gradually be provided by rolling back the plastic covering during the day, and eventually the cloches can be removed altogether.

CHAPTER 4

LAWNS

To Turf or to Sow?

You can create a lawn in one of two ways – either by laying turf or by sowing grass seed. Turf is offered for sale by specialist suppliers and is delivered pre-cut into conveniently sized rectangular sections. The grass is already growing in what, in effect, is a mat of soil – in fact, if you were to picture turves as carpet tiles you wouldn't be far off the mark. Grass seed is readily available from garden centres and specialist seed merchants. Both methods will produce an equally good-looking lawn. The table below outlines the main points to consider.

What will it cost?	Turf is much more expensive than seed
How much ground preparation is involved	Both require similar preparation
Is it hard work?	Depends on the soil. Turf is heavy to handle
When can the job be done?	Turf can be laid any time as long as the ground isn't frozen. Once turf is delivered, it must be layed immediately. The best times to sow are April/May and September/October
How long does it take to have a lawn?	Turf gives you an 'instant' lawn and can be used to the full in a couple of months. A sown lawn will begin to look good in a couple of weeks but shouldn't be used for four to six months

Preparing the Site

Whether turfing or sowing, all your efforts will be wasted unless the ground is thoroughly prepared beforehand. Lumpy land is one of the most common causes of unsightly-looking lawns – not least because the grass on the offending hummocks is invariably scalped by the lawnmower! So start the work well ahead of your chosen sowing or turfing deadline: that way there will be no danger of having to do a rush job because you've had unexpected demands on your time or been held up by bad weather.

Bear in mind that if you choose to lay turf in spring or summer and the weather is mild and dry, the turves will quickly deteriorate if they are left stacked up for more than forty-eight hours. It's therefore especially critical to have the ground ready and waiting when the turf arrives. However, if a delay of more than three days is really unavoidable, spread the turves out flat, with the grass facing upwards, on a sparse area of ground (ideally in the shade). Make sure that they are well spaced out and keep them well watered if the weather is dry.

To prepare the ground, proceed as follows:

1 Clear the site of builders' debris, bricks, large stones and so on.

2 When the soil is reasonably dry, dig over the whole area to the depth of a spade, removing any old tree stumps or roots and the worst of the weeds (if necessary, treat the area with a quick-acting weedkiller such as Weedol).

3 Make sure that the site is level: this is best done by eye, since some undulations are generally desirable. If you stand back, crouch down and squint across the surface, the high and low areas show up more clearly. Start by roughly levelling with the back of a fork.

4 Final preparation of the surface involves compacting the soil while maintaining a light, crumbly texture in just the top inch or so. Wait until the soil is fairly dry and start by treading systematically over the whole area, with your weight on your heels. Then scatter a dressing of Growmore at about 1 handful per sq m (yd). Next, rake over the surface at right angles to the direction in which you've been treading, filling in any depressions as you go and finally levelling.

Buying Turf

Whatever you do, be very wary of cheap offers of 'meadow turf' because, very often, that is exactly what it will be – virtually any old grass with a good proportion of weeds mixed into the so-called bargain! What you want is turf made up of proper lawn grasses, which has been regularly weed-treated, rolled and cut over the past year.

If possible, you should try to see a sample of the turf before buying (look for healthy colour, absence of weeds, good-looking grasses and uniform thickness of soil with plenty of roots showing).

A more expensive but extremely reliable, top-quality turf is available under the brand name Rolawn. This cultivated turf uses only specific lawn grasses (with absolutely no weeds) and is cut to a perfectly uniform thickness, making it easy to lay.

Calculate the area of ground to be turfed before you ring up for quotes. Knowing how many turves are required will allow the supplier to give you a firm price, including delivery. It also means that you can make instant comparisons between one company and another. Bear in mind that smaller-sized turves will be lighter and easier to handle.

Laying Turf

The turf will arrive either loosely folded or rolled up, with the grass to the inside. So that it isn't hanging around any longer than absolutely necessary, arrange to have it delivered when the weather looks like staying fine and when you can be sure of having enough spare time to lay it properly. Prior to delivery, earmark where the turf can be

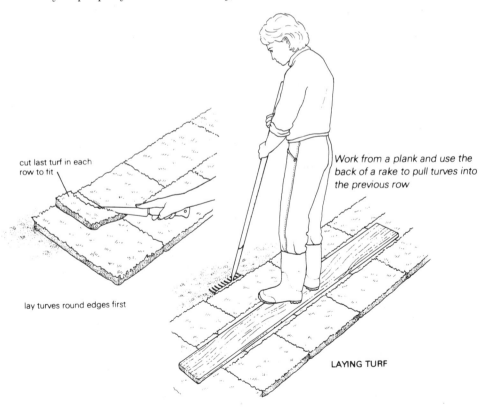

cut last turf in each row to fit

Work from a plank and use the back of a rake to pull turves into the previous row

lay turves round edges first

LAYING TURF

stacked so as to be as close to the site as possible. If it's simply dumped by the front gate, you'll be letting yourself in for a whole load of extra work.

What you'll need
- A wheelbarrow, if necessary, to carry the turf;
- A few planks of wood to stand/walk on as you work – otherwise you could damage the turf. Scaffold planks are ideal and can be hired;
- An old knife;
- A rake for tamping-down.

Step-by-step guide
1 Mark out the desired shape of your lawn with canes.
2 Start by laying a row of turves along the edge to mark the finished shape. Adjust them as you go to give a pleasing outline.
3 Then lay the first row, butting each turf against the next. When you get to the end of the row, lay the last turf over the edging turf you've already laid and cut it with the knife to fit. Then tamp down the row with the back of the rake.
4 Lay the second row of turves by working from a plank laid over the first row – this will also help to press the turf evenly and gently into the ground. When you've laid out the turves, pull them into the first row with the back of the rake.
5 Lay subsequent rows in exactly the same way until the whole area is covered. If you find a turf with a hole in it, patch it by simply pushing an appropriately sized piece of turf into the hole.
6 Then the most important job is to water. If the turves dry out, they'll shrink, so keep the sprinkler going little and often.

Choosing Seed

You can buy pre-packed grass seed either off the shelf of a local garden centre or by mail order from specialist suppliers. Both are reliable sources. As with turf, though, you can get different types of grass seed mixtures, depending on whether you want a fine, ornamental lawn, a tough 'utility' one, or something in between. You can even obtain mixtures that are specially selected for, say, a shady site or a problem soil. All you have to do is choose the one that best meets your requirements. You'll need about 25–40 g per sq m (1–1½ oz per sq yd).

Sowing Seed

Having bought the seed, you must wait for conditions to be right before sowing it. What you want is a fine spell of weather so that, after a day or two, the top inch or so of soil on your prepared site is fairly dry yet that underneath is still on the moist side. It would certainly be a mistake to attempt to sow seed on wet, muddy ground.

Step-by-step

1 Mark out the area to be laid to lawn with canes. Bear in mind, though, that you should sow an area a few inches bigger all round than you actually want in order to allow for final trimming and to give you a little leeway if the grass is rather sparse around the edges.

2 To sow the seed evenly, mark out 1 sq m (yd) and sprinkle 2 handfuls over it. That will give you an idea of what the correct rate looks like, and that's as accurate as you need to be. Then get two large plastic flower pots. Put one inside the other and turn them so that the holes align but are only half-uncovered. Fill with seed and shake it over the lawn. By twisting the inside pot you can effectively adjust the rate at which the seed comes out.

SOWING SEED

Use two large plastic pots – one inside the other – to hold the seed. By twisting the pots and shaking, you can easily control the distribution of seed at the correct rate.

Rake gently over surface with a spring-tine rake

3 There's no need to bury all the seed once it is sown. Simply rake over the surface very gently so that the seed is just partly covered. A spring-tined lawn rake is the ideal tool for the job.

4 The seed you bought will have been specially treated to deter birds from eating it. Nevertheless, it would be a wise precaution to cover the area with a network of criss-crossing cotton threads (stretched between sticks in the ground) a few inches above the soil's surface or with plastic bird netting. It will also help to make it a no-go zone for any dogs, cats or kids.

5 Within seven to fourteen days the young grass will be beginning to make a pretty good show. And if the weather has been dry, you can now water with a fine, gentle spray. Once the grass is around 7.5 cm (3 in) high, a light trim with a lawnmower will help to thicken it up, but remember not to let the lawn be used for other activities for at least six months.

Looking After Your Lawn

The lush, green British lawn is the envy of gardeners right around the world and it's all thanks to the great British climate – we might have cause to complain but the grass just loves it. And that is naturally very good news when it comes to looking after a lawn. As long as you are prepared to see to its basic requirements – which is only fair, considering the pleasure it gives – your lawn will invariably take any amount of punishment and come through unscathed.

All being well, then, maintenance of your lawn will involve just a few routine tasks. Some of these, like mowing, will need to be carried out on a regular basis during a particular season – others may need to be attended to only once or twice a year (see Chapter 12). None of them is particularly complicated, although they do require a certain level of understanding if the end result is to be successful.

When to mow

Mention 'frequency of mowing' to any gardener and the reply will undoubtedly be 'too blooming often!' In fact, the timing of your mowing is fairly critical and it can pay dividends by saving you a good deal of work in the course of the year. For example, the earlier you give the grass its first cut, the sooner you'll have to be out there every week mowing it!

Let's first look at the special requirements of new lawns. The first mowing should be done when the grass is about 7.5 cm (3 in) high.

Make sure that the blades of the mower are really sharp and adjust the 'height of cut' setting on the mower so that only the top 1 cm (½ in) of the grass is removed – that will probably mean choosing the highest setting. With each subsequent mowing, reduce the height of the cut until the grass is left about 1 cm (½ in) long.

In all but the mildest of winters, grass is dormant enough not to need cutting. When it starts to grow again in spring, the growth rate gradually increases, reaching its peak in summer, before it tails off again towards the approach of winter. Mowing generally starts, therefore, as soon as the grass is seen to be starting to grow – usually in March – and, at this time of year, once a week will normally be adequate. The same is true when the grass is slowing down in autumn. When the grass is growing rapidly, though – say, from May to the end of August – the keenest lawn buffs may want to mow twice a week.

It's important to bear in mind that while the main objective is obviously to keep the grass short, mowing on a regular basis also keeps the grass healthy. The worst thing you can do is leave it for several weeks and then give it a really drastic cut, within half an inch of its life. The shock to its system is very often just too much to bear! Grass should never be cut by more than about 1 cm (½ in) at any one go, and that's why lawnmowers have blades with height adjusters – as the grass grows more quickly, so the height of the cut can be slowly reduced. And it's also a mistake to think that a really closely mown lawn is necessarily going to be the most attractive. The height of the grass should be decided according to your type of lawn, as well as the season.

RECOMMENDED HEIGHT OF GRASS				
Lawn type	Spring	Summer	Autumn	Mild winters
Ornamental lawns	1-2 cm (½-¾ in)	0.5-1 cm (¼-½ in)	1-2 cm (½-¾ in)	2-2.5 cm (¾-1 in)
Utility lawns	2.5-3 cm (1-1¼ in)	2-2.5 cm (¾-1 in)	2.5-3 cm (1-1¼ in)	3-4 cm (1¼-1½ in)

How to mow

Mowing comes high on the list of least-liked jobs around the garden. Most of us, therefore, want to get the job done as quickly and efficiently as possible. To that end you want to choose the mower that best suits your requirements (see the above table) and get into the habit of adopting good mowing practice:

- Choose a time when conditions are right – preferably when the ground is firm and the grass is dry;
- Always pre-check the mower to make sure that it's in good working order;
- Scour the lawn for any debris, small stones, abandoned children's trinkets and so on;
- Scatter any wormcasts, using a stiff broom;
- Start by mowing round edges and into any tricky corners before proceeding to the main area. (If using an electric mower, always work away from the power point and take the recommended safety precautions);
- If you have a mower that makes stripes, work in straight lines, aiming to finish nearest to where the mower will be stored or can be easily carried away;
- Always remove grass clippings – only during a drought might it be worth leaving them on the lawn to help preserve moisture;
- Try to mow in the opposite direction each time. The easiest way to do this is to work diagonally across the lawn.

Watering

It seems that every time we settle down to enjoy a good, hot summer, within a matter of weeks we're being told to refrain from using hosepipes and garden sprinklers. In theory only, therefore, you should be ready to water your lawn as soon as there is a fairly prolonged dry spell, which could be any time from early May onwards. And try to do so before your lawn starts to show obvious sign of stress – fading to yellow, followed by drying out and browning.

The best time to water your lawn is in the evening – it's the same for all garden plants – and you should try to maintain a good, steady supply so that the water gets right down to the roots rather than merely tickling the surface. A hose and lawn sprinkler are essential.

Feeding

Just like any other plant in your garden, grass gradually uses up its fair share of goodness from the soil in order to stay alive and healthy. It's therefore necessary to give it an extra boost, especially when the grass is growing vigorously in spring. There are two sorts of lawn fertiliser available – one for spring, which contains extra nitrogen to encourage healthy leaf growth, and one for autumn, which has extra phosphorus to strengthen root growth. However, if you feed with the spring fertiliser in April and June, you shouldn't need an autumn feed.

AERATING   TOP DRESSING

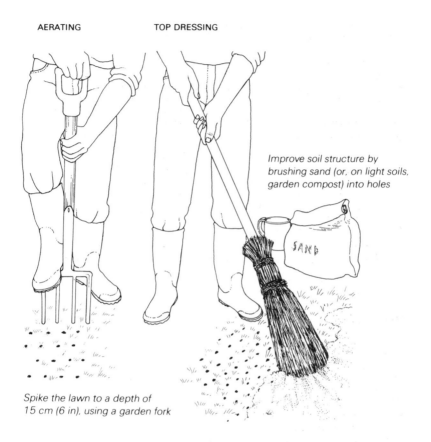

Improve soil structure by brushing sand (or, on light soils, garden compost) into holes

Spike the lawn to a depth of 15 cm (6 in), using a garden fork

Spring and autumn are good times to improve the structure of the soil in your lawn generally. 'Aerating' involves spiking all over the surface of the lawn to a depth of about 15 cm (6 in) with a garden fork. This will open up any compacted soil and let the air in. It's especially useful on badly drained soil. After spiking, brush in a dressing of sharp sand. On light soil use well-rotted garden compost or a mixture of soil and peat. This can then be worked deep into the lawn, using a stiff brush or the back of a rake, via the 'air holes' created by the aerating process. The combined techniques should be carried out several weeks before mowing starts in spring, and then again after mowing ceases in, say, October. Raking with a spring-tined rake will remove old, dead grass, encouraging the young grass to grow by giving it more light and air. It also removes a barrier to water, which will then be able to penetrate much more easily.

WHICH MOWER?

Electric	Petrol
☞ Furthest part of lawn must be within 60 m (200 ft) of power point ☞ You must be prepared to take necessary safety precautions ☞ Machines are light and easy to handle/manoeuvre ☞ Quieter in operation ☞ Minimal maintenance ☞ Small machines are much cheaper than their petrol equivalents ☞ Might not be powerful enough to tackle difficult conditions – e.g., very rough/long grass	☞ Free from external power source ☞ Only option if furthest part of lawn is more than 60 m (200 ft) from an electrical power point ☞ Machines tend to be more powerful than electric equivalents ☞ Can generally cope better with difficult ground ☞ Maintenance is time-consuming ☞ Noisy in operation ☞ Machines are heavy and can be cumbersome to manoeuvre ☞ More expensive

Cylinder	Rotary/Hover
☞ Capable of producing the finest, most ornamental cut ☞ Roller, if heavy enough, will produce sought-after stripes ☞ Won't cope as well with long/rough grass ☞ More awkward to manoeuvre ☞ Allows easier cutting up to edges ☞ A grass box is usually fitted as standard and collection tends to be more efficient ☞ Larger machines are more expensive than their rotary equivalents	☞ Don't give such a neat finish ☞ Can cope with difficult conditions, rough ground, etc. ☞ Hovers can reach awkward areas and cut long, wet grass ☞ Few rotaries have rollers and hovers can't have them ☞ Only certain models have efficient grass collection ☞ Electric machines require minimal maintenance ☞ Blades are simply replaced rather than sharpened ☞ Small, electric machines are the cheapest option of all

CHAPTER 5

PERMANENT ORNAMENTALS

Permanent planting schemes need careful consideration. Take your time to get to know a little about the plants you like and, ideally, visit other gardens for ideas. Before buying any plant you'll need to consider these points:

Site: The plant must suit the situation (sun/shade/shelter).

Soil: Make sure you can provide conditions to meet the plant's needs (mainly, does it require wet or dry soil, acid or lime?).

Size: Take into account the plant's ultimate height/spread and make sure there's room for it. Avoid having rows of plants of the same size together, although taller subjects will need to go to the back of the border unless they're being used as focal points.

Form: Make use of different shapes – upright, weeping, round – and use these selectively to create interesting arrangements and effective contrasts within groups.

Colour: Plan groupings so that delicate colours or subtle leaf markings are set off against darker foliage. Use bold colours sparingly to make a real splash. Aim to have adjacent plants giving of their best at the same time.

Arrangement: Try to arrange plants so that individual borders, or sections of border, make a complete picture – bear in mind that these might be viewed from different angles.

Spacing: Borders will look sparse at first if every plant is given sufficient space for its ultimate size. Still, don't be tempted to plant permanent plants closer. It's better to fill in the spaces with annuals until the permanent ones grow.

By arranging plants in groups, you can plan to have at least part of the garden looking its best at a particular time so as to create real impact and focus the attention – this is generally far more successful than having just a few high spots scattered all over the show. It will help, too, if you make use of the full range of permanent ornamentals on offer – trees, shrubs, roses, climbers and herbaceous perennials – all of which are dealt with in more detail over the following pages.

Bear in mind, finally, that the more evergreen subjects you can include, the more established your garden will look, especially in the 'quieter' months of the year – certainly avoid a concentration of deciduous plants in any one area. The tables below show how the main season of interest of the various subjects at your disposal can be considered alongside the special roles they might perform.

PERMANENT ORNAMENTALS FOR YEAR-ROUND INTEREST	
Season	Types of permanent ornamentals
SPRING/EARLY SUMMER	Early-flowering shrubs such as Mexican orange blossom, cotoneaster, broom, daphne, deutzia, forsythia, common lilac, spiraea, pieris, mahonia, rhododendron. Trees such as birch, hawthorn, laburnum, magnolia, flowering crab and cherry. Climbers like wisteria, hydrangea, clematis
MID-SUMMER	Roses – bush, standard and climbers. Herbaceous perennials like asters, astilbe, campanula, delphinium, dianthus, geranium, gypsophila, chrysanthemum, iris, kniphofia, dahlia, lavatera, phlox, salvia and many, many more
LATE SUMMER/ AUTUMN	Late-flowering/berrying shrubs – for example, buddleia, cotoneaster, hibiscus, hydrangea, hypericum, pyracantha, skimmia. Trees/shrubs for autumn foliage colour such as maple, berberis, birch, beech, hawthorn, pagoda bush. Climbers like bittersweet, Virginia creeper, grape vine
WINTER	Winter-flowering shrubs such as viburnum, winter jasmine, wintersweet, winter-flowering cherry. Evergreens with distinctive foliage – spotted laurel, elaeagnus, euonymus, holly, ivy, conifers. Plants with vivid bark, such as dogwood

How to use permanent ornamentals

Trees: Small or slow-growing trees can be used sparingly to add height in the border, create a focal point and cast dappled shade (position shade-tolerant plants underneath). Close-planted, suitable subjects will make screens/windbreaks.

Shrubs: Use to create mass effect and permanent structure – rather than have no two alike in a border, try to include a few of the same species to establish a theme and create impact. Also use as focal points (isolated) or as divisions/hedges.

Roses: For reliable show of colour/scent/form year in, year out. Make use of the different forms – bush, standard, climbers.

Climbers: Will provide vertical interest at eye level and can be used to cover trellis/pergolas/fences/walls and camouflage ugly views or give shelter/privacy. Evergreen types will form a useful backcloth, especially on perimeter fences.

Herbaceous perennials: Can be relied on to provide a colourful display from year to year, arranged to form either bold splashes of colour or subtle drifts. Require only routine care and attention but, because the top growth dies off in winter, confine them to group plantings among evergreen subjects so as to avoid having large bare expanses of border.

Buying the Plants

Unlike other plants you might choose to include in your garden, permanent ornamentals are supposed to be exactly that – permanent. However many others may come and go, it is these that will form the backbone of your garden design and mature over the years to establish its essential character. Buying healthy specimens, therefore – from a reputable supplier such as a nursery or garden centre – is of paramount importance if they are to last the course and give of their best. Be prepared, too, to spend money on them. For while the biggest isn't necessarily the best, very small specimens may be weak and difficult to establish. And the smaller they are, of course, the

HOW PLANTS ARE SOLD			
Type	**Time to plant**	**Pros**	**Cons**
Container-grown	All year round	No waiting for the right season to start planting	Sometimes slow to establish. More expensive
Bare-rooted	November/ March	Cheaper than pot-grown plants. Can inspect root system	Must be planted immediately. Plants vulnerable
Pre-packed	November/ March	Readily available and convenient. Often bargain price	Common varieties. Health of plant depends on how it's being stored. Generally poorer quality
Root-balled	Late spring/ early autumn	Can buy large plant cheaper than if pot-grown. Minimal root disturbance – will establish well	Ball mustn't dry out

longer they will usually take to have any real effect in the garden. You will also find that the less common varieties are generally more expensive. But just think that for the sake of a few extra pounds you can look forward to having something that bit different and of immense long-term value.

Trees and shrubs, together with most other types of permanent ornamentals, are displayed and 'packaged' in different ways, depending on how they have been grown and where they are being sold. In nurseries and garden centres they are either container-grown, bare-rooted (without soil but with the roots wrapped to keep them moist) or root-balled (the soil around the roots is retained and contained in a wrapping). In high street shops and supermarkets you will often find pre-packed plants, which are basically bare-rooted types presented in attractive, easy-to-display packaging. Each type has its pros and cons and will require slightly different treatment when it comes to planting.

How to recognise a healthy plant
Container-grown: The soil/root-ball should be firmly settled in the container and not at all loose. Fine roots growing out from the pot are a good sign – avoid those containers with surface roots or a thick root growing from the base. Look for even growth/form and healthy appearance of leaves and stems.
Bare-rooted: The plants must be dormant when you buy and plant them, so avoid any that show signs of leaf growth. Stems should be of uniform thickness and robust. Make sure that roots are strong and spreading and a good colour – not fine and white.
Pre-packed: As above but more difficult to inspect. Look to general condition of display to judge whether plants are being cared for – warm conditions could spell dry roots and premature growth on plants. Look at the packs very closely.
Root-balled: Inspect the wrapping to make sure that it isn't torn and feel the root-ball to see whether it's moist or not. Plant should have a good shape and, if evergreen, a strong, healthy leaf colour.

Preparing to Plant

Since permanent ornamentals are going to be having their feet in the ground for a very long time, it's vital that you prepare the planting sites thoroughly by digging over the soil and adding quantities of garden compost, well-rotted manure or peat (see Chapter 2). This should be standard practice, whether you're planting up an entire border or simply making a home for a single rose. Never just prepare a hole in uncultivated land since it will then act like a sump and the plant will be left standing in water. As for the method of planting, it's not so much the nature of the plant that determines how this is done as the type of material – namely, whether it's container-grown, bare-rooted, pre-packed or root-balled. For this reason any specific requirements the various types of ornamentals might have will be dealt with later on under the appropriate heading.

Planting bare-rooted and pre-packed ornamentals

Bare-rooted and pre-packed ornamentals are treated in exactly the same way – hardy subjects should be planted in late autumn, more tender plants in spring. The ground should be neither frozen nor waterlogged and if planting has to be delayed (this should never be for more than a few days), the plants should be stored in a frost-free place with the roots kept covered and moist.

1 Use canes to mark out the planting positions in the border, checking that they are spaced according to your plan and the plants' requirements.

2 Unwrap the plants and soak the roots in a bucket of water for several hours. Take this opportunity to judge the depth and spread of the roots so that you can prepare planting holes of a suitable size.

3 Dig out the planting holes, making them big enough to allow the roots to be well spread out.

PLANTING BARE-ROOTED TREES AND SHRUBS

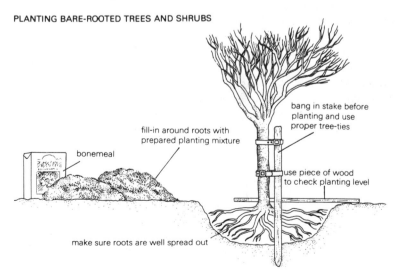

bang in stake before planting and use proper tree-ties

fill-in around roots with prepared planting mixture

bonemeal

use piece of wood to check planting level

make sure roots are well spread out

4 Prepare a planting mixture by adding an equal amount of garden compost or peat and a handful of bonemeal to the soil you have dug out.

5 If stakes are required (see 'Aftercare', page 59), bang these in before planting, hammering each one deeply into the ground towards the centre of the hole on the windward side. Stakes for trees should come a third of the way up the stem and the tree should be tied to them with special plastic tree-ties. Never use wire or nylon string, which will cut into the bark.

6 Once the plants have been well soaked, prepare them for planting by trimming back any extra-long roots and removing weak/damaged shoots.

7 Set the roots in the planting hole and check for size/depth, making adjustments as necessary. A piece of wood laid across the top of the hole will help to indicate the soil level, and the plant should be planted at exactly the same level as in the nursery.

8 Start to fill in around the roots with the planting mixture and settle the soil down by gently shaking the plant. Add some more soil and firm this down with your hands. Continue to fill the hole, little by little, firming in the soil with your foot but not treading too hard.

Planting root-balled and container-grown ornamentals

Root-balled and container-grown ornamentals have similar requirements but can be left for several weeks if ground conditions aren't right for planting – for example, if the soil is particularly wet, cold or

PLANTING CONTAINER-GROWN AND ROOT- BALLED TREES AND SHRUBS

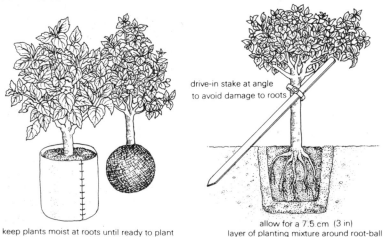

drive-in stake at angle
to avoid damage to roots

keep plants moist at roots until ready to plant

allow for a 7.5 cm (3 in)
layer of planting mixture around root-ball

frozen. Both must be kept moist at the roots, though, so make sure that the containers are well watered and that root-balls are either plunged in damp soil/peat or sprayed with water. The plants should stay in their containers/wrappers right until the moment of planting.

1 Prepare the planting holes and mixture first, as described for bare-rooted plants (page 57). Each hole should be large enough to accommodate a root-ball with some 7.5 cm (3 in) to spare around the sides and underneath. The top of the root-ball (or base of the stem) must be level with the surrounding soil once it has been firmly planted.

2 Put a 7.5 cm (3 in) layer of planting mixture into the holes, put in the plants – still in their containers/wrappers – and check for height. Make adjustments as necessary and replace the plants.

3 Carefully cut away the pots (these are usually fairly thin and flexible) or wrappers, taking care not to damage or break up the root-ball. Pots and wrappers must be removed completely.

4 Fill in around the soil balls with the prepared planting mixture, firming it down as you go.

5 If the plant needs staking, bang the stake in at an angle to avoid damaging the root-ball.

Aftercare

Certain permanent ornamentals are a good deal less demanding than others and so if a low-maintenance garden is your main priority, it would make sense to go for those subjects that will thrive and put on a good show with minimal attention. Of course, trees, shrubs, roses, climbers and herbaceous perennials all require slightly different methods of cultivation – we'll be looking at their specific requirements later on – and each group has its fair share of fussy and not-so-fussy characters. However, you must still be able to satisfy even the most easy-going plant's basic needs (in terms of site and situation) and be willing to take the appropriate steps to keep it happy. Generally, such routine care involves just a few of the simple tasks outlined below.

Pruning: Bare-rooted shrubs should have their stems/branches cut back by one third of their length immediately after planting. Container-grown and root-balled plants shouldn't require any immediate treatment. For specific pruning requirements once plants are established, refer to the individual plant's cultivation details. Generally, the purpose of pruning is to: (a) remove old, dead, damaged wood; (b) keep the plant within bounds and in shape; and

(c) encourage flowering. You are bound to grow many plants that require regular pruning, so buy a good pair of secateurs.

Training/support: Training will be required for certain climbers (to encourage the branches to spread attractively over the wall/fence, they are tied in to fixed wires/trellis) and for some shrubs, such as roses or fuchsias, if you want to achieve a 'standard' form (a bushy head atop a main stem). Support is sometimes necessary to keep tall-growing plants upright (with canes, as used for dahlias) and to stop clumps of spreading plants with drooping stems from falling on to the ground (gather them up within garden twine wrapped around a few sticks or use a proprietary plant-support frame). Amazingly, many of the tallest-growing ornamentals need no artificial support at all.

Weeding: It's especially important to keep the immediate area around newly planted trees and shrubs completely free of weeds as they will only compete for the valuable nutrients and moisture in the soil. This is also why trees and shrubs planted in a lawn should have a good area of bare soil around their base for at least the first few years. Regular hoeing, just below the surface, will help to control persistent weeds – use this technique in conjunction with mulching.

Mulching: A layer of peat/garden compost/well-rotted manure is placed around the plants (not touching the stems), usually in late spring, to conserve moisture, keep down weeds and give the plants/soil a boost for the season ahead. In winter it will help to protect the roots of frost-sensitive subjects. Grass clippings are beneficial but to a slightly lesser extent.

Feeding: The recommended application of a slow-acting fertiliser like bonemeal at planting time will sustain young plants until their relatively undeveloped root systems become established in the ground. Most permanent ornamentals will also benefit from a routine spring feed, either in the form of a mulch or a proprietary fertiliser (see Chapter 2). However, refer to your plants' specific cultural requirements.

Watering: Newly planted ornamentals need to be thoroughly watered in, which will mean several trips to the tap with the watering can or the use of a hose. The same copious watering is necessary whenever there is a dry spell, especially in the first few years, because the plants' roots will not yet have reached deep enough to find any extra reserves of moisture.

Protection: Young trees and shrubs, especially evergreens and more tender subjects, may need some protection from wind, especially in exposed gardens. So, if you're planting in November, be prepared to erect a windbreak. You can buy suitable perforated plastic material at the garden centre and this should be supported on strong stakes to the windward side of the plants. Large, staked trees might need further anchorage against winds – use two or three 'guy ropes' tied around the main stem (protect the bark by providing a cushion of rubber or plastic hosepipe between it and the rope/twine) and secured to pegs in the ground.

Trees and Shrubs

In smaller gardens avoid tall-growing trees with heavy, spreading canopies because, apart from blocking out the light and casting shade, they will look totally out of proportion once mature. However, taller subjects with a narrow, columnar habit are perfectly suitable, as are more delicate trees that won't prove so overpowering. When considering the ultimate height and spread of a tree, you also have to take into account whether it is a slow/medium/fast grower. Generally, the best advice is to go for one or two medium-sized yet fairly fast-growing specimen trees, which will grow no taller than about 7.5 m (25 ft), and use smaller species and taller-growing shrubs to add height within borders.

You can calculate the space required between two trees by adding together their ultimate heights and dividing by two (varieties of the same type, used for screening, can be closely spaced). For shrubs, add together the spread of adjacent subjects and divide by two. If planting a sizeable tree near a perimeter fence, first make sure that your neighbours know what you're doing. Legally, they could have a tree removed if it blocks out too much light and they can certainly lop off any branches overhanging their garden. It's a good idea, too, to keep even quite small trees a reasonable distance from the house, especially if your soil is heavy clay.

Top ten trees
Maple (Acer): There are many varieties of this large group, covering a range of leaf colours from deep red, through pink to bright yellow, plus many variegated forms. Some have superb bark colouring too. Look especially for A. griseum, with peeling cinnamon bark, and A. capillipes, with bark like a snake's skin.
Silver birch (Betula pendula): White, peeling bark and, in spring, yellow catkins. The variety 'Youngii' is dome-shaped with weeping branches and reaches about 3.5 m (12 ft). Deciduous. Soil: not

critical. Site: sun/slight shade. Pruning: cut out dead wood in spring.
False cypress *(Chamaecyparis lawsoniana)*: While there are various
compact types for the shrub border and also some real monsters,
'Fletcheri' is a useful medium-sized variety – it reaches 2 m (6 ft) after
ten years – for use as a specimen plant or as hedging/screening.
Feathery, grey-green foliage. Evergreen. Soil: well-drained. Site: not
exposed. Pruning: trim to shape in spring.
Hawthorn *(Crataegus monogyna)*: The native hawthorn, growing to
about 4.5 m (15 ft) with scented, white flowers in spring, red berries
in autumn. A more compact form is *C. oxyacantha* 'Rosea Flore
Pleno' with double pink flowers. Deciduous. Soil: not fussy. Site:
sun/slight shade. Pruning: Remove dead diseased wood in winter.
Juniper *(Juniperus)*: The incredibly thin, upright conifer, *J.
virginiana* 'Skyrocket', with soft blue-grey foliage, makes a startling
specimen tree, growing to 4.5 m (15 ft) or more in time. Evergreen.
Soil: not fussy. Site: sun/semi-shade. More compact juniper
varieties are ideal for borders. Pruning: none needed.
Flowering crab *(Malus)*: Various worthwhile varieties, mostly reaching no more than 4.5 m (15 ft) in height. 'Liset' has red flowers in
spring and red/purple fruits; 'John Downie' has white flowers/
orange-red fruits; and 'Golden Hornet' has white flowers/bright yellow fruits (lasting into December). Deciduous. Soil: add extra
humus. Site: sun. Pruning: in winter, tidy up tree by removing dam-
aged/ill-placed shoots.
Flowering cherry *(Prunus)*: There's a wealth of superb varieties,
most of which reach about 6 m (20 ft) when fully grown. Some are
weeping, others spreading or with a narrow, upright habit.
Unusually, *P. subhirtella* 'Autumnalis' bears white or pink flowers
right through winter. Cheal's weeping cherry, with pink flowers in
spring, has very pendulous branches. Deciduous. Soil: well-drained/
slightly alkaline. Site: sunny. Pruning: cut-out damaged shoots in
late summer.
Ornamental pear *(Pyrus)*: Few varieties are widely available,
although you will find *P. salicifolia* 'Pendula' fairly easily, which is
reminiscent of a weeping willow but with attractive, soft grey foliage.
Reaches about 7.5 m (25 ft). The cream/white flowers in spring followed by inedible fruits are relatively inconspicuous, but it's well
worth growing for the foliage alone. Deciduous. Soil: not fussy. Site:
prefers full sun. Pruning: cut out dead/damaged wood in winter.
False acacia *(Robinia)*: Its delicate golden-yellow foliage belies its
tough constitution. The variety 'Frisia', eventually reaching about 7.5
m (25 ft), is best for domestic gardens. Deciduous. Soil: any. Site: any

but not too windy. Pruning: cut out old/damaged wood in summer.
Mountain ash/whitebeam *(*Sorbus*)*: While many varieties of this
tree can grow into giants, the smaller ones include *S. aucuparia*
'Fastigiata' (columnar, up to 4.5 m/15 ft) and 'Joseph Rock' (which
has superb autumn foliage and yellow berries). With white flowers in
spring, they provide interest for the best part of the year. Deciduous.
Soil: not fussy. Site: sun/semi-shade. Pruning: cut out dead/dam-
aged branches in winter.

Top ten shrubs
Barberry *(*Berberis*)*: Of the many and varied varieties available, the
mound-forming evergreen, *B. candidula*, is particularly noteworthy
for its mass of bright yellow flowers in May. The dwarf deciduous
'Nana' variety has dark bronze foliage that turns red in autumn. Soil:
any. Site: sun/slight shade. Pruning: to tidy – trim evergreens after
flowering, deciduous types in February. Buy container-grown
plants.
Butterfly bush *(*Buddleia*)*: Easy-going and valuable for late summer
colour – flowers attract butterflies. *B. davidii* has various varieties
with colours ranging from purple-red to violet-blue, plus white.
Responds to some attention, especially pruning. Some are semi-
evergreen. Quite different is *B. alternifolia*, the fountain buddleia,
which has arching stems with clusters of flowers along their length.
Soil: well-drained. Site: prefer sun. Pruning: in March, cut back previous season's growth to within 5 cm (2 in) of old wood.
Cotoneaster: This is grown primarily for its vivid berries and rich foliage colour in autumn. Most useful for ground cover is the low-growing, deciduous fishbone cotoneaster, *Cotoneaster horizontalis*. Of the
evergreen types, *C. conspicuus* 'Decorus' is a superb, compact shrub.
All have relatively insignificant, usually white flowers in spring. Soil:
not fussy. Site: sun/slight shade. Pruning: not necessary.
Elaeagnus: A tough, easy-going evergreen shrub, grown for its distinctive variegated green/bright yellow foliage – invaluable in the
darker days of winter and ideal for exposed sites. *Elaeagnus pungens*
'Maculata' is the common one, although there is also the attractive *E.
ebbingei* with leaves that are silvery-white underneath. Soil: not
fussy. Site: sun/slight shade. Pruning: not necessary. If grown as a
hedge, trim at the beginning and end of summer.
Euonymus: Evergreen varieties are similar to elaeagnus, having
similarly striking variegated foliage. For low-growing ground cover,
choose varieties of *Euonymus radicans*, while for a bushy, specimen
shrub go for *E. japonicus*. The deciduous types, the spindleberries,

are grown for their autumn foliage and berries and make large shrubs or trees. Soil: any. Site: full sun for pronounced variegation. Pruning: not necessary, but don't mind being cut hard back.

Fuchsia: The hardy garden fuchsias will grow into sizeable bushes and reward you with delicate pink/mauve/purple flowers from mid-summer through to autumn. They may suffer in hard frosts but will usually recover come spring. *Fuchsia magellanica* 'Versi-color' is particularly noteworthy as it also has variegated leaves. Deciduous. Soil: fairly rich, moisture-holding. Site: sun/semi-shade. Pruning: in March/April, cut shoots back to within 2.5 cm (1 in) of the ground for strong, new growth.

Hebe *(*veronica*)*: A valuable group of evergreens, the common ones making neat, compact bushes with glossy oval leaves, many flowering from mid-summer through to late autumn – for example, the medium-sized 'Autumn Glory', with vivid violet blooms. Some varieties have quite different leaf shapes (even conifer-like) and flower forms/colours. Smaller-leaved varieties are the hardiest. 'Carl Teschner' is a low ground-hugging variety with violet flowers in June/July. Soil: well-drained. Site: sun/slight shade. Pruning: not necessary – can tidy in early summer. (Choose hardiest varieties in cold/northerly districts.)

Mahonia: A common shrub but nonetheless valuable for year-round interest – evergreen holly-like foliage, bright yellow, scented spring flowers and black berries in autumn. The low-growing *Mahonia aquifolium* is especially valuable for its foliage – bronze in autumn, purple in winter. *M. japonica* is tall-growing (2 m/6 ft), as is the superb *M.* × *media* 'Charity' with flower spikes from mid-winter. Soil: any. Site: shade (ideal under trees). Pruning: if the stems start to become bare, cut back in spring.

Thuja: An invaluable family of conifers with several dwarf varieties that make striking specimen shrubs. *Thuja occidentalis* 'Rheingold' has feathery golden foliage which turns copper/bronze in winter. *T. orientalis* 'Aurea Nana' has dense, erect, golden-yellow foliage and forms a distinctive, rounded bush – it, too, turns bronze in winter. Soil: well-drained. Site: sunny. Pruning: not necessary.

Viburnum: This group of plants alone can provide all the year-round interest you could possibly want. Grow *Viburnum bodnantense* for clusters of scented white flowers on bare stems throughout winter, the striking evergreen *V. burkwoodii* for large, fragrant, white flowers in spring, and *V. davidii*, also evergreen, for bunches of blue berries in autumn. Soil: add extra humus. Site: sun/slight shade. Pruning: not necessary – tidy up deciduous types after flowering.

Roses

Roses are sold as either bare-rooted or container-grown plants and should be planted as described on pages 56 onwards. And while their aftercare consists of the same routine tasks as other permanent ornamentals – watering, mulching, feeding and so forth – they do have certain specific requirements, especially when it comes to pruning. On planting, usually in March, large-flowered and cluster-

PRUNING ROSES AND OTHER SHRUBS

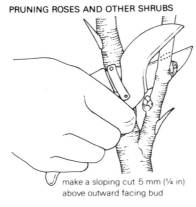

make a sloping cut 5 mm (¼ in)
above outward facing bud

Type	Description	Spacing	Aftercare
Large-flowered bush (hybrid tea)	Bush and standard forms. Long stems; single, well-shaped, medium/large blooms	Small: 45 cm (18 in) Medium: 60 cm (2 ft) Tall: 1 m (3 ft)	Stake standards. For large blooms, remove side buds. Dead-head flowers
Cluster-flowered bush (floribunda)	Flowers in clusters, opening over long period. Petals tend to be looser	As above	Stake standards and tall-stemmed bushes. Dead-head flowers
Shrub (including miniatures)	Modern and old roses, usually taller and broader. Less formal	Shrubs: half of ultimate height. Miniatures: 30 cm (1 ft)	Trim to shape as necessary
Climbers (including ramblers)	Large blooms on stiff stems (or clusters of blooms on pliable stems); often flower twice in a year	45 cm (18 in) from wall/fence; climbers 2 m (6 ft) apart, ramblers 3 m (10 ft)	Train from outset to wind up posts/fan out on walls as above

flowered bush roses – formerly known respectively as hybrid tea and floribunda roses – need to be cut hard back: bushes to within 10–15 cm (4–6 in) of the ground, standards to within 20 cm (8 in) of the main trunk and ramblers to about 30 cm (12 in).

Once they are established, the pruning of bushes and standards involves removing dead/damaged/overcrowded wood and cutting back the remaining stems to about half their length in early spring (always make an angled cut above an outward-facing bud). However, on cluster-flowered bush roses the previous season's shoots from the base should be just lightly pruned ('tipped') and only very old wood cut hard back. The treatment of climbers and ramblers varies but, generally, pruning involves removing old/weak wood and cutting back side shoots that have flowered to about 7.5 cm (3 in) of the main stem – this should be done in late summer/autumn.

Top ten roses
All roses prefer a sunny, sheltered situation. Soil should be rich in humus, neutral/slightly acid and well-prepared.

Large-flowered bush roses (hybrid teas)
'**Ernest H. Morse**': Masses of vibrant-red, strongly scented, large blooms that aren't prone to damage from rain. Medium height. Upright growth and dark-green foliage. Fairly disease-resistant.
'**Grandpa Dickson**': Perhaps one of the finest yellow varieties. The perfectly formed blooms have long, lemon-coloured petals, sometimes tinged with pink at the edges. Medium-sized, upright habit with dark, glossy leaves. Free-flowering, late into the season, slightly scented and very sturdy/disease-resistant.
'**Just Joey**': Flame-red/copper petals, ruffled at the edges, make this one stand out in a crowd. It forms a medium-sized bush and the stunning, fragrant flowers are set off against dark matt green foliage. Very reliable, flowering into autumn, and quite trouble-free.

Cluster-flowered bush roses (floribundas)
'**Amber Queen**': A perfect subject for group planting in borders, this has a bushy yet compact habit and is very free-flowering, bearing clusters of large, amber-yellow blooms with tightly packed petals. It has a good scent and is also fairly resistant to disease.
'**Margaret Merril**': A beautiful white rose with well-formed flowers and a strong, sweet fragrance, making a medium-sized bush. The blooms are prone to damage from rain and disease-resistance is only fair, but it's hard to beat for form/scent.

'*Pink Parfait*': With a branching habit, the long, smooth stems bear masses of soft-pink blooms, the petals flushed cream at the base. Medium-sized, its lack of scent is more than compensated by its free-flowering nature, good disease resistance and the resilience of its flowers, which are excellent for cutting.

Shrub roses
'*Frau Dagmar Hastrup*': A name to reckon with but a rose that has much to recommend it – single pink, beautifully scented blooms, which flower right through the season, set against dense, dark green foliage, with a mass of large, red hips in autumn. Forming a fairly tall (1.2 m/4 ft) and broad (1 m/3 ft) bush, it is one of the more compact Rugosa roses and is very resistant to disease. Also ideal for an ornamental hedge.

'*Red Blanket*': As its name implies, this is a superb, low-growing, spreading shrub that can be used for ground cover. Semi-double, rose-red flowers are borne in clusters, which stand slightly above the mat of glossy, dark green foliage. Free-flowering and scented.

Miniatures
'*Angela Rippon*': Not reaching more than 30 cm (12 in) high, this bushy yet compact variety, with pale carmine-pink double blooms, is ideal for group planting at the front of borders. Blooms have a reasonably strong scent and the plant is extremely free-flowering.

Climbers
'*Zéphirine Drouhin*': The thornless rose is a very old variety yet nonetheless a great favourite with its extremely strong scent and glowing, pink-red blooms that are semi-double and beautifully formed. It will bloom in flushes from June onwards (if dead-headed) and can either be encouraged to climb or pruned back to form a tall shrub.

Climbers

Some climbers are self-clinging and, as such, attach themselves readily to walls, fences and so forth. Others, however, can climb only by twining their stems or tendrils around some form of support, which is usually provided by means of wires or trellis. Make sure that planting sites are thoroughly prepared with the plants positioned some 45 cm (18 in) away from the base of the wall/fence/pillar.

Bare-rooted plants should have their roots spreading away from the wall. Pruning requirements vary considerably, so check this when choosing plants. Bear in mind, too, that even self-clinging types often need some initial support to encourage them to climb.

Top ten climbers

Actinidia: Two quite different deciduous climbers bear this name – one is the Chinese gooseberry (*Actinidia chinensis*), with massive heart-shaped leaves that will clothe a wall in no time (grow both male and female plants if you want edible fruit). The other, *A. kolomikta*, is purely ornamental with smaller leaves that are flushed pink/cream when grown in a sunny situation. Soil: not fussy. Site: sun/semi-shade. Support: yes. Pruning: tidy up in winter.

Clematis: Also known as virgin's bower, this massive family of delightful climbers is mostly deciduous. Wide-ranging flowering periods and flower forms/colours. 'The President' is a large-flowered, purple variety, blooming from June to September. 'Jackmanii Superba' has huge, deep purple flowers, while 'Nelly Moser' is soft pink striped with deeper pink. *Clematis tangutica* bears small, lantern-like, lemon-yellow flowers in summer. Soil: rich in humus, well-drained. Site: sun/shade at roots. Support: yes. Pruning: varies according to variety.

Ivy (Hedera helix): Ivy is invaluable for year-round cover and you can choose from a host of varieties, each with distinctly different leaf forms and variegations. 'Goldheart' is brightly splashed with yellow, while 'Buttercup' is an all-yellow variety. They'll cling to practically any surface and won't damage walls if these are in good repair. Soil: any. Site: sun for variegated types. Pruning: tidy plants in spring and summer.

Hydrangea: May take a few seasons to get established, but *Hydrangea petiolaris* eventually provides impressive cover with its massive white flower-heads from June to late summer against a mass of fresh green foliage. Deciduous. Best against a wall or sturdy structure that will take its weight. Soil: well-drained/slightly acid. Site: sun/slight shade. Support: self-clinging but needs encouragement. Pruning: not necessary – tidy up in winter.

Jasmine (Jasminum): If you can provide it with a warm, sheltered situation, the white jasmine will reward you with fragrant white flowers from mid-summer through to September. Go for *J. officinale* 'Grandiflorum'. *J. nudiflorum* produces yellow flowers in winter. Soil: not fussy. Site: sun/shelter. Support: yes. Pruning: tidy up after flowering.

Honeysuckle *(*Lonicera*)*: Less demanding than clematis. The scented blooms can be enjoyed from mid-summer into early autumn. It is a bushy, vigorous grower and should have space to run a bit wild. *L. japonica* includes both deciduous and evergreen varieties, 'Halliana' having highly fragrant clusters of white flowers turning to yellow in summer. Soil: well-drained. Site: sun/partial shade. Support: yes. Pruning: tidy after flowering.

Virginia creeper *(*Parthenocissus*)*: *P. quinquefolia* is the real Virginia creeper, while *P. tricuspidata* is commonly called Boston ivy. Both will provide superb russet-red hues in autumn. Of special value, though, is the variegated form, *P. henryana*. Soil: fairly rich, well-drained. Site: any. Support: in early stages of growth only. Pruning: tidy up in spring.

Passion flower *(*Passiflora caerulea*)*: All you need is a warm, sunny, sheltered wall to be able to enjoy this most exotic of all climbers with its dramatic, sculptural white/purple flowers, some 7.5 cm (3 in) across, from mid-summer through to September. Protect from frost in winter – plants that are slightly damaged usually recover. Soil: well-drained. Site: full sun. Support: yes. Pruning: cut back damaged/unwanted growth in spring.

Ornamental grape vine *(*Vitis*)*: While some varieties do bear edible fruits, these are grown primarily for their vivid autumn foliage colours. *V. vinifera* is the less vigorous species and the variety 'Brant' is recommended for its crimson/pink/orange leaves and purple grapes in autumn. Soil: well-drained/slightly chalky. Site: sun/partial shade. Support: yes. Pruning: trim back in summer.

Wisteria: One of the most traditional climbers, which will give of its best only if properly cared for. Choose the less vigorous *Wisteria floribunda* for impressive lilac-blue flowers in early summer. Soil: well-prepared/add humus. Site: full sun. Support: yes. Pruning: cut back new growth (side shoots) to about 15 cm (6 in) after flowering.

Herbaceous Perennials

This group embraces all those favourite flowering plants that have always been part and parcel of the traditional garden border. And while many can be raised from seed (see Chapter 3), those that are required for permanent planting, to provide a display year in, year out, are more often bought as bare-rooted or container-grown plants. In theory, you can plant the latter at any time, but herbaceous perennials are best planted when dormant, either in spring (March) or autumn – just as long as the ground isn't frozen or waterlogged. Plant in groups of three to five plants (as space allows) so as to create real impact. Special requirements regarding aftercare include:

- Providing canes/plant-support frames for tall-growing subjects in early summer before growth starts to accelerate;
- Dead-heading flowers on a regular basis;
- Lifting and storing the root systems (tubers) of certain frost-sensitive subjects, such as dahlias and begonias, in autumn;
- The division of spreading/large clumps, in autumn or spring, to create several smaller ones for transplanting elsewhere in the garden;
- Cutting back top growth at the end of the season (usually November) to within 15 cm (6 in) of the ground.

DIVIDING HERBACEOUS PLANTS

lever clumps apart using two forks back to back

Almost without exception, herbaceous perennials should be planted in properly prepared, well-drained ground (add plenty of organic matter) that is in sun or partial shade.

Top ten perennials
Aster/Michaelmas daisy: For a mass of lavender-pink, blue or white flowers at the front of a border, try the low-growing (23 cm/9 in) *Aster alpinus*. For later flowers on tall stems (1 m/3 ft), *A.* × *frikartii* is probably the finest of all, flowering profusely for some three months.
Astilbe: Best planted in large groups where the feathery flower plumes, reaching some 1 m (3 ft) high, can form subtle drifts of colour – choose ones that blend well. 'Spinel' is a superb salmon-red, flowering in June/July. Dwarf varieties are also available.
Campanula: With charming, soft blue, bell-shaped flowers throughout summer and distinctive, strappy foliage, the genus includes low-

growing (30 cm/12 in) types like *Campanula carpatica* 'Blue' and the white-flowered *C. barbata* 'Alba', as well as *C. latifolia* varieties reaching some 1 m (3 ft).

Chrysanthemum: *Chrysanthemum maximum* is the most common, traditional species. *C. indicum* 'Charm' forms dense, 45 cm (18 in) high mounds of starry, scented flowers in shades of red, pink, orange, yellow and white. A superb, tall-growing, double pompon type, *C. koreanum*, flowers early in cooler conditions and continues right through to autumn.

Dahlia: A host of different flower forms, plus tall-growing and dwarf varieties, all usually at their best in August/September and lasting until the first frosts (when foliage is blackened, lift tubers and store for winter). Cactus-flowered types have a mass of narrow, pointed petals; the flowers of pompon varieties have a rounded, honeycomb appearance; others are single- or double-flowered, many with a central collar of smaller petals in a contrasting colour.

Delphinium: Look for the *Delphinium* × *belladonna* hybrids with blue, violet or white, tightly packed flower spikes in early/mid-summer, capable of reaching up to an amazing 1.5 m (5 ft). 'Blue Bees' is a beautiful sky-blue.

Pinks *(*Dianthus*)*: 'Mrs Sinkins' will keep its mound-forming silver foliage through the winter and provide scented, double flowers (pink with a deep mauve eye) through the summer. *D. plumaris* 'Old Laced Pinks' is slightly lower-growing (30 cm/12 in) with frilly flowers (double and single) in every shade of pink. Ideal for chalky soil.

Baby's breath *(*Gypsophila*)*: Invaluable to the flower arranger and also a charming border subject, the delicate flowers in fine, loose sprays, look like a haze of white cloud in drifts some 1 m (3 ft) high. 'Bristol Fairy' has lovely double blooms, flowering from June to September.

Iris: The most usual one, but nonetheless stunning, is *Iris kaempferi*, with large white, blue or purple flowers in early summer rising from erect, strap-like leaves. *I. pallida* 'Variegata' makes a superb specimen plant with sky-blue flowers and cream/green-striped foliage. Both will grow to about 1 m (3 ft). (Lift and divide after flowering.) The flag iris (*I. germanica*) is well known. Available in many colours, it produces tall spikes of flowers in summer. Give it a sunny spot.

Red-hot poker *(*Kniphofia*)*: *K. erecta* is a giant with its poker-shaped flower spikes of flaming orange-red reaching up to 1.2 m (4 ft), surrounded by strappy leaves in a rather wild clump. 'Bressingham Comet' is somewhat more restrained yet equally impressive, with flame-yellow flowers in September/October.

CHAPTER 6

HOW TO USE ANNUALS, BIENNIALS AND BULBS

You might well be thinking that if you were to follow the recommendations in the preceding chapter and make full use of all the immensely valuable permanent ornamentals, there would be precious little room left in your garden for anything else – indeed, you could even be questioning the need for any further additions. But the sort of plants we will be describing in this chapter play a quite different role, which is especially useful in the new garden where the permanent plants will take time to give of their best.

The beauty of annuals, biennials and bulbs is that they are comparatively cheap and extremely cheerful. Between them they will put on an almost immediate show, from early spring to late summer, and ask for very little in the way of care and attention in return. And because they embrace such an enormous diversity of plant forms and colours, they can be put to work in all manner of situations to serve a variety of purposes. Bear in mind, however, that while many bulbs will come up year after year, annuals and biennials die after flowering.

Traditionally, and especially in parks and large estate gardens, these plants would be relied on to provide the main seasonal display. The borders would come alive with colourful bulbs in winter/early spring, to be followed by a spring/early summer show of biennials, with a carpet of annuals taking their place from summer through to autumn. Then the biennials would go in again and so the cycle would continue. And while this, in theory, is how these plants are used to provide seasonal colour and interest, our approach will usually be rather less rigid.

Automatic and total replacement of one group of plants with another calls for impeccable timing and, in the case of annuals and biennials for immediate effect, the raising of a considerable quantity of plants to the 'planting-out' stage under cover (see Chapter 3) or in a seedbed elsewhere in the garden. So rather than aiming for a continuous display across an entire border, it makes sense (and is in any case far more effective) to have key areas giving of their best at a particular time so that there is always something going on. And, as you will see, this is extremely easy to achieve if you use permanently planted bulbs together with annuals and biennials that are both sown outside where they are to flower and bought in as young plants – or, if convenient, ones raised under cover yourself.

Annuals

The main season of interest for both hardy and half-hardy annuals (see Chapter 3) is from about June through to September/October, after which the plants are scrapped, leaving vacant ground that can be used for planting, say, bulbs or hardy biennials or for sowing some of the hardier annuals for a slightly earlier display the next year. But the fact that annuals are 'disposables' doesn't mean that they should be relegated to the lower ranks of plant society. Indeed, you need look no further than the sunflower to see that while their lifespan may be short, they can still put on a most amazing show.

Annuals, then, are capable of making tremendous growth – whether it be upwards or outwards or both – and of producing flowers, often in profusion, over a surprisingly long period of time (especially when compared to many perennials). It will probably come as no surprise, however, that the quality of their performance – as with all plants – depends entirely on their state of health and general well-being. And your responsibilities in this respect start long before the plants are given their respective homes in the garden.

A good start in life is essential, and whether you are raising annuals from seed yourself (see Chapter 3) or leaving the job to the nurseryman, the end result should be sturdy young plants ready for planting out when the time is exactly right. The most common mistake – and often a fatal one for the plants – is to plant far too early. Some of the retail outlets are to blame here because, come the first sunny weekend of the year, perhaps as early as April, they are only too willing to part with their plants. It doesn't seem to matter to them that a frost might strike the very same night and kill the lot!

Late May is the earliest you should consider planting half-hardy and tender annuals – commonly referred to as 'bedding plants' – and only then if you are reasonably certain that the frosts are well and truly over. With hardy annuals, of course, even the seed can withstand frosting so the planting time for these isn't so critical. In all cases, though, avoid buying plants that are tall and spindly as this usually means they have been forced into growth prematurely and will be too exhausted to make a full recovery.

While the range of plants at your disposal is truly vast, selection can be made a lot easier by considering the way in which they might best be used. As you will note from the following table, some lend themselves better to certain situations than others:

Situation	Recommendations
Mass plantings/ ground cover	Go for just a few different varieties, all with a fairly uniform habit of growth, strong foliage, simple flower form and similar colour range - decide on a theme for the planting and stick to it
Dot plants/ focal points	Here you want an isolated plant, or group of plants of the same variety, with particularly bold flowers or distinctive foliage. Can be used within shrub borders or in containers (see Chapter 9)
Filling small spaces	Pockets of earth at the edge of the border and all around the garden (even between paving stones or bricks in walls) can be filled with creeping/trailing/mat-forming types. Aim for an informal effect and avoid edging with alternate colours!
Screening and wall cover	Use quick-growing climbing annuals to scramble up walls, fences, trees, trellis screens, the sides of old sheds/ outbuildings, etc. - try sweet peas, nasturtium, canary creeper or morning glory

It makes sense to raise the plants required for mass plantings from seed as you'll get the required number a good deal more cheaply. And if you were to restrict these to hardy annuals, you could get them off to an early start, sowing them outside where they are to flower. A tip here would be to arrange the areas to be sown in such a way that the young seedlings/plants won't be glaringly obvious. This would probably mean sticking to taller-growing varieties that can go to the middle/back of the border or be tucked between lower-growing permanent ornamentals. Bought-in half-hardy plants could then be placed at strategic positions – say, towards the front of the border – to provide immediate interest while the seed-raised plants are reaching maturity.

If you grow plants from seed, you will find advice regarding the final spacing/thinning of plants on the seed packet. With bought-in plants, guidance in this respect is not always forthcoming, although the individual displays should be clearly labelled with a full description of the subject (always double-check the flower colour and habit of growth/height) and details of cultivation. This will certainly be the case if you buy from a reputable source and, what's more, there will be experts on hand to give advice if you are in any doubt. As a rule of thumb, planting distances should be the equivalent of the ultimate spread/width of the individual plants.

Certainly, when it comes to planting, you should avoid arranging your plants in serried ranks (see 'Sowing flowers outside', page 32). And to get the plants off to the very best start, you should make sure that the soil is reasonably fertile, with a good crumbly texture, and free of weeds. Deep digging isn't necessary for annuals, although organic matter in the soil will help to retain moisture in dry spells. Almost without exception, annuals prefer a position in full sun or partial shade. More tender subjects need to be fairly sheltered.

Planting container-grown annuals

The plants you buy will probably be growing in a polystyrene tray divided into individual cells, each of which holds one plant. The trays can be split up to provide you with 'strips' of the required number of plants, although the minimum is normally four or five. Just as common are offerings of four or five plants in moulded plastic units, while larger or more mature subjects – like geraniums, say – will be in individual pots. If planting has to be delayed once you get the plants home, keep them in a sheltered spot outside and ensure that they don't dry out. Ideally, plant as soon as possible.

1 Sprinkle a very light dressing of fertiliser – about a handful per sq m (yd) – over the planting area and rake it in. Don't overdo it or you'll finish up with all leaf and few flowers.

PLANTING BOUGHT-IN BEDDING PLANTS

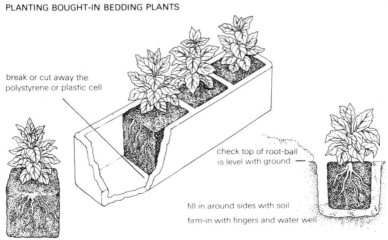

break or cut away the polystyrene or plastic cell

check top of root-ball is level with ground

fill in around sides with soil

firm-in with fingers and water well

remove root-ball so that it remains intact

2 Before removing a plant from its container, have a planting hole ready – this should be dug out with a trowel and be 1 cm (½ in) or so bigger on all sides than the root-ball of the plant (look at the size of the cell/pot).

3 Plants in flimsy plastic or polystyrene cells can be removed by cutting/breaking away the material or by pushing up through the drainage holes. Those in individual pots will need to be carefully eased out – support the plant with one hand while you turn the pot upside down and give it a firm tap to loosen the root-ball, which should be a solid mass of soil/roots.

4 Put the root-ball in the planting hole so that the top is level with the surrounding ground. Fill in around the sides with earth and firm down around the base of the plant with your fingers.

5 Proceed in the same way with each plant and water in thoroughly.

Aftercare

Most important, especially in the early stages of growth, is to keep the plants well watered and the ground around them completely clear of weeds – do this by hand and by careful hoeing. Always water in the evening (when the sun has lost its strength) and do so copiously – just wetting the surface is really worse than useless.

All annuals should be dead-headed as soon as blooms begin to fade, so make a daily inspection and the plants will reward you by flowering in profusion. Taller plants with a branching/spreading habit of growth might need staking and tying in to keep them looking neat and tidy and to stop them getting knocked about by wind or rain. Lower-growing, straggly subjects (such as petunias) can be trimmed back a bit if they get too wild towards the latter half of the season. Also at about this time you could apply a general liquid fertiliser to give the plants an extra boost. Annuals tend to be little troubled by pests and diseases. Slugs can cause serious damage, especially to young plants, so try any of the standard methods – bait, traps and so on – to keep them under control. Very often, however, the only solution at the end of the day (literally) is to pick them off the soil/plants by hand. The other most common pests are greenfly and blackfly, which must be controlled (or preferably prevented) by routine spraying with a systemic insecticide.

Top ten annuals

Snapdragon (Antirrhinum): Half-hardy annual. While dwarf (15 cm/6 in) and medium-height (30 cm/1 ft) varieties are available, the tall varieties (45–75 cm/18 in–2½ ft) are subjects for the middle/back of the border where they will put on a dazzling show if planted in fairly dense groups. Old-style flower forms have been joined by fully double and trumpet-shaped blooms in a wide range of single colours and bi-colours.

Begonia: Half-hardy annual. It is the fibrous-rooted varieties of *Begonia semperflorens* that will provide a carpet of colour, with masses of sturdy little pink/red/scarlet/white flowers above bushy mounds of foliage, generally no more than 15–20 cm (6–8 in) high. Use towards the front of border – groups of several plants are needed to create impact.

Larkspur (Delphinium): Hardy annual. This is the annual version of the delphinium and can be easily raised from seed in the middle or at the back of the border where many varieties will reach as high as 1 m (3 ft). The tightly packed flower spikes come in shades of soft blue, pink, lilac and violet, as well as white. Sow/plant in a group or a meandering double row.

Geranium (Pelargonium): Half-hardy perennial, often treated as an annual. Specimen plants with bold flowers, distinctively marked foliage and a uniform habit can be used singly as dot plants amongst foliage/evergreen subjects or in containers (see Chapter 9). Lower-growing, compact varieties (15–30 cm/10–12 in high) are best planted in groups to the front/middle of the border.

Busy Lizzie (Impatiens): Half-hardy annual. Like the begonia, this low-growing beauty has to be used in mass plantings if it is to make a real show. Plants of single and mixed colours, as well as bi-colours, are available – in a wide range of both brilliant and pastel shades at the pink/red/orange end of the spectrum, plus white. A particularly valuable plant for shady areas as it dislikes hot, dry conditions.

Sweet pea (Lathyrus odoratus): Hardy annual. Sow these 2 m (6 ft) giants (in March/April) where they can be given support with canes/ netting or wires against a fence/wall. They'll quickly put on wonderful shows of colour and provide superb cover/screening. Indispensable for a cottage-garden effect and also for cut flowers (pick regularly to prolong flowering).

Mallow (Lavatera): Hardy annual. Just two or three of these bushy plants in a single group will make a superb focal point with their showy, glowing pink or purest white flowers smothering the stems and the less significant foliage from mid-summer through to late September/early October. Average height: 60 cm (2 ft). Easy to raise from seed.

Lobelia: Half-hardy annual. No collection of annuals would be complete without the ubiquitous lobelia – and with good reason. Confine the trailing varieties to hanging baskets/windowboxes and choose the upright/compact edging types for the front of the border. Here they will form a stunning blue (various shades) or white carpet from early summer through to September. There are also bronze-leaved varieties.

Petunia: Half-hardy annual. Avoid those with a branching/pendulous habit, which are best displayed in tubs and hanging baskets, and choose varieties of the Multiflora or Floribunda type that make a more compact plant suitable for the front of the border. Plant several in a group for a riot of colour (pink, red, violet, white) all summer long.

French marigold *(*Tagetes*)*: This half-hardy annual looks superb in mass plantings either to the front (dwarf types) or middle of the border – most reach 30–45 cm (12–18 in) high. Various flower forms – fully double, frilly, honeycomb, single, crested – in every imaginable shade and combination of yellow/gold/orange/red.

Biennials

The only difference between annuals and biennials is that the latter are planted out as young plants in late summer/early autumn to flower in spring/early summer the following year (refer to Chapter 3 if you want to raise the plants yourself from seed). Otherwise they should be treated in exactly the same way as annuals and – because there are just as many different plant forms, flower colours and so on – should be selected and positioned within the border with equal care. As the plants will be developing during the winter months, aftercare won't involve such close attention to watering. Nevertheless it's important to make sure that they don't dry out, especially immediately after planting.

Making use of biennial subjects in addition to annuals and bulbs means you can have colour in the garden virtually all year round. However, it does call for a fairly strict rotation of plants. Being 'disposables', biennials are traditionally cleared from the border in early summer to make room for the summer-flowering annuals (which, in turn, have to be removed in time for the young biennial plants to be planted out in autumn). Be warned, however, that you will have to harden your heart when it comes to consigning certain subjects to the compost heap as, very often, the plants are still putting on a reasonable show.

If you were to leave biennials until they came to the end of their useful life, they would be occupying valuable ground that could be filled far more effectively with those subjects that are designed for a summer display – namely, annuals. What's more, as the season progresses, you'll see the plants deteriorating by the day, which isn't a happy sight. One way of making the scrapping of plants a little less painful would be to lift the ones that are strictly speaking hardy perennials (the daisy, *Bellis perennis*, for example, and the polyanthus) and split up the root systems to create several smaller plants. Those with healthy, young growth could then be planted in a spare piece of ground, out of direct heat/sun, to spend a quiet summer until you are ready to move them back into the border in autumn.

You will find some of the smaller biennial subjects (for example, pansies, polyanthus and primroses) being offered for sale in spring, very often already in flower. While this is a more expensive way of buying them – it's always cheaper to buy young plants that haven't been grown on under cover in a nursery – they can prove invaluable for adding an instant splash of colour, especially in the new garden. Bear in mind, finally, that the soil/site requirements of biennials are more variable than those of annuals. While some might thrive in average soil in full sun, for example, others could want a heavier soil in shade. So before making your final selection, be sure that you can provide the appropriate conditions.

Top ten biennials
Daisy *(*Bellis perennis*)*: Superb subject for mass planting at the front of the border, with cheerful, bobbing flower heads in shades of red, rose and white, just 15 cm (6 in) or so off the ground. Soil: fertile. Site: sun/slight shade. Planting distance: 20 cm (8 in).
Canterbury bells *(*Campanula medium*)*: Delightful bell-shaped flowers – in shades of pink, blue, mauve and white – tightly packed on strong stems reaching up to 1 m (3 ft) high. *C. pyramidalis*, the chimney bellflower, will grow a foot or so taller and has broad flower spikes of violet-blue or white. Soil: normal. Site: sun/slight shade. Planting distance: 23–30 cm (9–12 in).
Wallflower *(*Cheiranthus*)*: No spring display would be complete without the beautiful colours and fragrance provided by the wallflowers. Plant taller ones (38–45 cm/15–18 in) in groups towards the middle of the border, with dwarf types (18–30 cm/7–12 in) in sweeping bands along the front edge. Soil: normal/alkaline. Site: sun. Planting distance: 23–30 cm (9–12 in); dwarfs closer. Remember that when you plant wallflowers in the autumn they have more or less finished growing, so buy big plants.

Sweet William (Dianthus barbatus): A favourite old-fashioned flower that is sweetly scented and comes in glowing shades of pink and red. The blooms are tightly packed on compact plants, which generally reach about 45 cm (18 in) high. Plant in groups towards the front/middle of border. Soil: normal/alkaline. Site: full sun. Planting distance: 23–30 cm (9–12 in).

Foxglove (Digitalis purpurea): Few plants will put on such a spectacular display at the back of the border, with pink/purple flower spikes growing as high as 1.2 m (4 ft) or more. This native wild flower can be raised from seed or bought in as plants, but remember that it needs plenty of space. Soil: normal. Site: semi-shade/shade. Planting distance: 60 cm (2 ft).

Honesty (Lunaria annua): A flower arranger's delight and also a sight to behold in the border with its scented purple and white flowers followed by the distinctive flat, silvery seed-pods like so many fluttering discs of paper. At 60 cm (2 ft) high, it makes a perfect dot plant in the middle of the border. Soil: normal. Site: sun/slight shade. Planting distance: 45 cm (18 in).

Forget-me-not (Myosotis): Borders can be transformed into a sea of blue in early spring (a perfect foil for bulbs) by mass-planting this low-growing favourite (traditionally an edging plant). Pink and mixed colours are available for ringing the changes. Soil: add extra humus. Site: sun/semi-shade. Planting distance: 15–20 cm (6–8 in).

Iceland poppy (Papaver nudicaule): A superb subject that will create a haze of brilliantly coloured (pink/salmon/carmine/yellow/orange), delicate flowers atop long, slender stems. At 60 cm (2 ft) high, it's ideal for mass-planting in the middle of the border. Left in the border it will flower through the summer. Soil: normal. Site: sun/semi-shade. Planting distance: 20 cm (8 in).

Polyanthus (Primula): Like the pansy, this is a hardy perennial that can be treated as a biennial. The neat, compact plant is perfect for the front of the border/edging where the richly coloured flowers will form a perfect bouquet amidst the bright foliage. It tends to suit formal schemes best. Soil: moist, heavy. Site: shade/semi-shade. Planting distance: 15–23 cm (6–9 in). Lift and divide after flowering.

Pansy (Viola): While this is strictly a hardy perennial, it is best treated as either an annual or biennial. For early flowering from winter through to spring, the Universal pansies are the ones to go for. Available in a wide range of colours/bi-colours, these will provide a dazzling display and should be mass-planted at the front of the border for full effect. Sow seed under cover. Soil: add extra humus. Site: full sun/slight shade. Planting distance: 15–20 cm (6–8 in).

Bulbs

One of the greatest joys of inheriting an established garden is being taken by surprise, come the first spring, when the borders suddenly erupt with colourful flowering bulbs, apparently appearing from nowhere. In fact, the same unexpected pleasure can be experienced even when you plant bulbs in the garden yourself, for not only might you forget what you planted where but, as the years go by, you will probably find that those left undisturbed are quietly multiplying and spreading themselves over an increasingly wide area. The latter, which is referred to as naturalisation, is what happens in the wild – for example, where a woodland floor is carpeted with bluebells – yet it is only really desirable in smaller domestic gardens when confined to lawns. Here a host of charming subjects, such as dwarf daffodils, crocus and fritillaries, can be left to run riot. And because they'll be putting on a show before the grass starts into active growth, you needn't worry about having to manoeuvre around them with the mower.

By far the most common homes for bulbs, though, are borders and containers, where they are used as part of a planned display. Not that this implies any necessity for formality – as you will see, a row of tulips standing like so many soldiers on parade isn't going to do them, or your garden, a great deal of justice. Indeed, the arrangement and grouping of bulbs should be considered in exactly the same way as other types of garden plant and, primarily, be in keeping with the character of the garden (see Chapter 1). Certain subjects should be mass-planted, others look better springing up singly from, say, a mat of ground-hugging evergreen foliage. And taller types, of course, will have to take their place behind more diminutive species.

Perhaps most important of all, though, is a carefully planned colour scheme, for the brilliance or subtlety of colour of a chosen bulb will be all but lost if it is thrown in amongst madly clashing neighbours. Very often the most effective device is to stick to a simple combination of perhaps just two basic colours for each area of planting – for example, blues/yellows, reds/mauves, pinks/cream/white. There are no hard-and-fast rules, of course, but it's usually preferable to be able to enjoy a display without first having to reach for your sunglasses! Make sure, finally, that the bulbs you are selecting for a particular arrangement will be in flower at the same time. In fact, by choosing varieties really carefully, you can plan to have the individual displays providing a succession of colour, from as early as January through to May.

Buying the bulbs

The golden rule here is to buy your bulbs the moment they first appear in the shops/garden centres because you will then be getting them at their healthiest. Bulbs need to be stored in cool, dry conditions, and the longer they're sitting on the shelves, the more likely they are to deteriorate if conditions aren't just right. Inspect the bulbs for the following signs:

Healthy bulbs to buy	Unhealthy bulbs to avoid
The bulbs should be firm with the outer skin intact. They should be displayed in cool, dry conditions. If being sold loose, choose the biggest ones with the fewest blemishes	Any soft bulbs, especially around the base plate (where the roots will grow from). Avoid those with roots/shoots and ones displayed in warm conditions

It will always pay to buy the best you can afford since cheap bulbs will be of little long-term value. You should also resist bargain offers and hand-outs from friends because, apart from not really knowing what you've got, they might be diseased. However, some of the special offers from reputable suppliers for bulk buying are usually a very good investment indeed and often include an excellent mixed selection. On this point, though, it's vital that all the bulbs you buy are clearly labelled – not just with the name but also with the flower colour. When buying bulbs loose, make sure that varieties from adjacent troughs aren't getting mixed up.

How to plant

As with any planting scheme, it's a good idea to plan on paper first so that you can come up with successful arrangements/groupings and have a reasonable idea of where the various subjects are to go in the border. You should also prepare the ground thoroughly and, seeing that bulbs are best planted as soon as possible after purchase, it would be advisable to do this well in advance. Dig the soil over, removing any plant debris and weeds, and add some organic matter/peat to help retain moisture. If using well-rotted manure, make sure that this doesn't come into direct contact with the bulbs. Once the ground is ready, you can proceed as follows:

1 Plant with a trowel or, if you feel like splashing out, a special bulb planter – this is like a deep, circular pastry cutter with a handle on top, which removes a complete plug of soil.

2 Dig out a hole that will allow the bulb to be at the correct 'planting depth' when it's sitting in the bottom. The distance is measured from the base of the planting hole/bulb to the soil surface and it's vital you get it right because bulbs have critical requirements – plant too deep and the bulb may not have enough energy to push its way to the surface; plant too shallow and the stems may topple over. (See 'Top ten bulbs' below for general guidelines in this respect – for specific varieties, check the recommended planting depth given on the labels or in the bulb catalogues. As a rule of thumb, plant 3 times as deep as the 'height' of the bulb.

3 If drainage needs to be improved, add a little coarse grit to the base of the planting hole before inserting the bulb (with the more pointed end pointing upwards!) and firming it down. Fill around the bulb and to the top of the hole with soil and firm the surface (replacing turf if you're planting in the lawn).

4 Proceed in the same way for all your bulbs, making sure that you keep to the recommended planting distances – both for depth and width apart. As general rule, aim for informal groups that intermingle slightly at the edges.

PLANTING BULBS

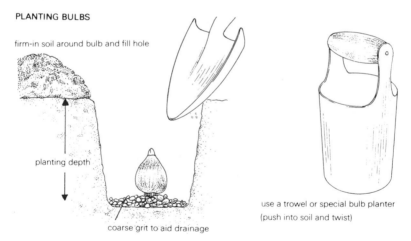

firm-in soil around bulb and fill hole

planting depth

coarse grit to aid drainage

use a trowel or special bulb planter
(push into soil and twist)

Aftercare

Keep the ground around the bulbs free of weeds. In spring apply a top-dressing of bonemeal to the soil, and once the bulbs are flowering feed once a week, at the recommended rate, with a liquid fertiliser that is low in nitrogen. After flowering, wait at least six to eight weeks before cutting off the foliage and never, never tie the leaves of daffodils into knots. After a few years it may well be necessary to lift, divide and replant over-large clumps and this should be done once the leaves have died down.

If you have to remove bulbs from the border completely in order to make way for other plants (it's usually possible to plant around them), lift them with the leaves intact and replant them close together in a shallow trench in a corner of the garden. This gives the leaves the opportunity to help build up the bulb for next season.

Top ten bulbs

These can be planted between September and November, directly into borders, to provide a display from mid-winter to late spring.

Crocus: The smaller-flowered varieties of *Crocus chrysanthus*, although most often grown in pots, look stunning when planted in an isolated group within the border. 'Cream Beauty' is a real gem with its open, cup-shaped blooms and another is 'Ladykiller' with slender purplish blue, edged with white flowers. The larger-flowering varieties, such as 'Pickwick' with the most beautiful lilac stripes and gold stigma, flower slightly later in February/March. Plant 7.5 cm (3 in) deep and 7.5 cm (3 in) apart in a sunny/sheltered situation.

Winter aconite *(Eranthis hyemalis)*: This buttercup-like, yellow-flowered bulb, growing just 10 cm (4 in) high with distinctive foliage spreading 7.5 cm (3 in) across, appears at the same time as the snowdrops, for which it makes a perfect companion. Plant 2.5 cm (1 in) deep and 7.5 cm (3 in) apart in sun/slight shade, preferably in fairly rich, well-drained soil.

Fritillaria meleagris: These are charming subjects for planting in natural drifts, especially in grass where their delicate, drooping, bell-shaped flowers can be seen to best advantage. They vary in colour from dark purple to white, and are chequered all over. There may be several flowers per stem which generally reaches 25–38 cm (10–15 in) high. Plant 7.5 cm (3 in) deep and 13 cm (5 in) apart in sun or shade. In the wild these plants are found in damp meadows, but they will grow in most reasonably moist garden soils.

Snowdrop *(Galanthus nivalis)*: A welcome sight as early as January and often lasting till March. There are both single- and double-flowered varieties, many with particularly distinctive green markings on the pure-white petals. Unlike most other bulbs, these are best bought as plants in pots or directly after flowering as green plants. Plant in natural drifts and informal groups, 10 cm (4 in) deep and 7.5–10 cm (3–4 in) apart. Best in slight shade. Ideally, leave in ground.

Dutch hyacinth *(Hyacinthus)*: While most often associated with indoor display, Dutch hyacinths are really effective when mass-planted in borders. They grow about 23–25 cm (9–10 in) high with 15 cm (6 in) flower spikes packed with either single or double 'bells', all of them scented. 'Blue Magic' has particularly impressive flower heads, while 'Chestnut Flower' is salmon-pink. Plant 15 cm (6 in) deep and 10 cm (4 in) apart, not in full sun.

Iris *(varieties of* Iris reticulata*)*: With typically iris-like flowers up to 7.5 cm (3 in) across on stems just 15 cm (6 in) high, this is a wonderful subject for mid-winter/early spring colour, especially in the rock garden. The flowers are a vivid violet and strongly scented. Plant 7.5 cm (3 in) deep and 5–7.5 cm (2–3 in) apart in a light, dryish soil in sun/semi-shade.

Grape hyacinth *(*Muscari*)*: As its common name suggests, this delightful bulb has delicate flower heads that look like a cross between a bunch of grapes and a hyacinth. Growing up to 25 cm (10 in) high, it is best left in the ground where it will quickly multiply. Flowers are scented and come in shades of vivid/soft blues, mauves and white. Plant 7.5 cm (3 in) deep and 10 cm (4 in) apart in a sunny position.

Daffodil *(*Narcissus*)*: Myriad varieties, some flowering as early as the beginning of March, others appearing at the end of April. Also a massive range of colour combinations and flower forms, including traditional trumpet, large- and small-cupped, double and orchid. There are so many, in fact, that narcissus are categorised in divisions, from 1 (trumpet) to 10 (wild types). For scent, look for the Jonquil, Tazetta or Poeticus types. Planting depth varies according to variety but for average-sized (5 cm/2 in) bulbs it is 13–15 cm (5–6 in). Plant five per 930 sq cm (1 sq ft) in slight shade.

Scilla campanulata: This is the cultivated bluebell and is a far more reliable subject for the garden than the wild species. The plants are generally low-growing (13 cm/5 in) and are perfect for mass-planting among shrubs where they will put on a colourful show (white and pink varieties are also available) in March. 'Spring Beauty' is a rather larger (20 cm/8 in), very sturdy and long-flowering variety. Plant 5 cm (2 in) deep and 10–15 cm (4–6 in) apart in sun/semi-shade and moist soil.

Tulip *(*Tulipa*)*: Depending on variety, tulips will flower from March to mid-May. Like daffodils, there are so many different types/flower forms that they have been categorised in divisions (from 1 to 14). For early flowers, try the Fosteriana (oriental) and Kaufmanniana (low-growing) ones, followed by Early Single and Early Double types, which are very sturdy and ideal for bedding. Mid-season varieties can then be followed by the latest-flowering Darwin and Cottage types. Plant 10–15 cm (4–6 in) deep with five per 930 sq cm (1 sq ft). Choose a sunny site.

CHAPTER 7

VEGETABLES

In most gardens, setting aside some ground for the growing of vegetables is high on the list of priorities, although the kitchen garden will invariably have to play second fiddle to the ornamental one – unless, that is, your main concern is to be totally self-sufficient. The space at your disposal, therefore, will generally be fairly limited, which means you have to be all the more selective when it comes to planning which crops to grow. This chapter concentrates on those vegetables that are best suited to the smaller kitchen garden and are easily raised from seed. Don't make the mistake of thinking you'll never set foot inside a greengrocer's again!

We've already discussed the main factors to consider when choosing vegetable varieties to grow from seed (see Chapter 3). You'll have seen that third on the list was 'space available' – and this is where you have to make a realistic assessment of:

- The ground area a given crop is going to occupy;
- The length of time it will be there;
- The time of the year it will be growing.

That way, you can start to draw up a master plan, which can be combined with a growing calendar. Earmark first of all the crops you think are 'musts', for whatever reason, and mark down where these would be best positioned and also the months of the year when they would be occupying the ground – from sowing right through to final harvesting/clearing. You may decide at this point to revise your list if a particular vegetable is hogging too much space. You will see, for example, that we haven't included potatoes in this chapter simply because they take up so much room in a small plot.

As you consider each vegetable in turn, bear in mind the feasibility of spreading the cropping season by growing early and late varieties. Take into account, too, the appetites and tastes of the family – you don't want a glut of any vegetable that can't be either eaten straight away or stored. Once you have accommodated the so-called mainstay vegetables, you can see where the gaps are and set about finding other crops to fill them. Variety, after all, is the spice of life both in the kitchen garden and in the kitchen.

The table opposite sets out the main tasks involved in growing your own vegetables.

TASK LIST FOR VEGETABLE GROWING	
Task	**Comments**
Buying seed/plants	Always check that the variety is suited to the conditions, the growing method and the season. If buying in young plants, make sure that they're healthy and can be planted immediately, at the appropriate time
Preparing the ground	All crops want a well-dug, fertile soil (see Chapter 2). Pay attention to specific needs, though, and take them into account when planning
Thinning	Seedlings should be thinned as soon as they can be handled. Don't delay the job or the plants will be severely weakened
Transplanting	Some plants hate any disturbance, others will tolerate it – avoid shocking them too much by transplanting only in favourable conditions (i.e. on damp, overcast days)
Weeding	Crops that don't like to be disturbed will need hand-weeding – otherwise use a hoe carefully. Don't leave the debris lying around
Feeding	Fertilisers are essential prior to sowing and sometimes as a top-up during the growing season. Normally use Growmore and with some crops (like tomatoes) use liquid feed during the season
Watering	All vegetables like consistently moist ground, so water well and often, especially when they are reaching maturity/ripening
Harvesting	Most vegetables are best when picked young and tender – don't grow more than you can cope with at a time. Short rows are preferable

Beans

An increasingly overwhelming variety of beans is popping up in greengrocers and supermarkets, on plates in restaurants, and in a good many kitchen gardens. But the three most popular ones, and also the most reliable in the British climate, will always be the broad bean, the French bean (or *haricot vert*) and the runner bean, which must be the run-away favourite. All appreciate a sunny site and thrive best in soil that is both fertile and free-draining, so make sure plenty of organic matter has been dug in the previous autumn. The most troublesome pest that affects them is blackfly, which cluster on the stems and cause damage to all parts of the plant – if you spot any, spray immediately with a proprietary insecticide designed to control aphids on vegetables.

Broad beans

Varieties	Description
Longpod	Pods are long and skinny. Hardy plants – can be sown in autumn in mild areas for early June harvest – and high-yielding
Windsor	Shorter, wider pods and more sweetly flavoured. Sow in spring only
Dwarf	Small pods on sturdy, low-growing (45 cm/18 in) plants. Ideal for exposed sites and growing under cloches

Sowings can be made in February under cloches for an early June crop and, without protection, in March and April for harvesting from the end of June to early September. Sow the seed 5 cm (2 in) deep and 15 cm (6 in) apart in twin rows – that is, two rows, or drills, with just 23 cm (9 in) between them. Keep weeds away from the young seedlings by careful hoeing. Tall-growing varieties will probably need some support – stretch string between stakes on either side of the crop. As soon as you see the first sign of pods forming, by which time the plants will be well in flower, remove the top 7.5 cm (3 in) of the stem by cleanly snapping it between your fingers – this, called 'pinching out', encourages early cropping as well as affording some protection against blackfly. Harvest pods when quite young and they can be eaten whole. For shelling, wait until the pods are swollen from the pressure of the mature beans within.

French beans

Varieties	Description
Flat-podded	The type traditionally grown in Britain with flat pods that are quite wide and prone to stringiness when allowed to mature. Pick when very young
Pencil-podded	New varieties with round, narrow pods, which are invariably stringless. Many are hardier than the flat types and generally more succulent

Sow in April under cloches to start picking by the end of June. Outside, sow in May and June for harvesting from July to early October. Seed should be sown 5 cm (2 in) deep and 10 cm (4 in) apart, in rows 45 cm (18 in) apart. Keep weed-free and support climbing varieties with twiggy sticks or netting stretched between stakes. Once plants are flowering, if weather is dry, water well and often – especially when pods are forming. Always pick when young – about 7.5–10 cm (3–4 in) long.

Runner beans

Varieties	Description
Stick	The traditional climbing varieties, reaching about 3 m (10 ft) in height. Many new ones are stringless. Flower colour can be pink/red/white (also bi-colours)
Dwarf	Limited varieties but ideal if space is limited. Plants (45 cm/18 in high) need no support. Lower but earlier yields

Runner beans cannot be sown outside until late April to late May depending on where you live. They'll provide a harvest from August to October. Plants raised under cover in pots in late April can be transplanted by the end of May (or after frosts) for picking by the end of July. Outside, sow seed 5 cm (2 in) deep and 30 cm (1 ft) apart in twin rows 45 cm (18 in) apart. Each plant will need a cane for support

SUPPORTING RUNNER BEANS

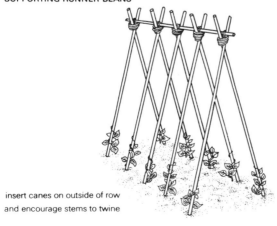

insert canes on outside of row
and encourage stems to twine

– insert these a few centimetres away from the seedlings along the outside of the rows. Angle the canes to meet at the centre, tying each pair together at the top to form a 'tent' framework. Tie canes between these, as a ridge, to keep the whole thing stable. As the plants develop, they may at first need a little help to twist round the canes, but will soon manage themselves. Once pods start to form make sure that the plants are well watered. Pick regularly, before they get tough and to encourage new ones to form.

Beetroot

The key to having tender, juicy beetroot throughout the summer is to grow small quantities in succession – that way, they won't get tough and woody through being left too long in the ground. Remember, too, that you can grow beetroot for storage, freezing and pickling for a year-round supply. The plants like a sunny site and fertile soil – sandy soil is the ideal. Add well-rotted organic matter to the ground well in advance of sowing.

Variety	Description
Globe	The most popular and common type of beetroot, with average-sized, round roots – red, yellow or white. Early and late varieties extend harvesting
Cylindrical	Few varieties generally available – will keep well for storage. Tend to have bigger roots

SOWING UNDER CLOCHES FOR EARLY CROPS

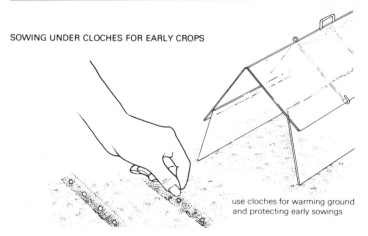

use cloches for warming ground and protecting early sowings

Make a first sowing of globe varieties under cloches in early March for a crop by the end of May/early June. Sowings outside at four-week intervals between mid-April and the end of June will provide a regular supply through to the end of September, perhaps even longer. Sow seed of cylindrical varieties for storage in late May/early June for lifting in October. Each beetroot 'seed' is, in fact, a fruit comprising a cluster of seeds. Soak them in water overnight to help germination and then sow in drills, where the plants are to grow, spacing the clusters 10 cm (4 in) apart for early crops, 20 cm (8 in) apart for later ones. Allow 20–30 cm (8–12 in) between rows. Thin by removing all but the strongest seedling from each 'seed' position.

Broccoli

The most popular types are purple-sprouting broccoli, which is harvested in winter, and calabrese, a summer and autumn crop. Like all brassicas, broccoli needs a rich, firm soil, which should have lime added to it in winter if it's on the acid side. A sunny site is best.

Varieties	Description
Purple-sprouting	Hardy varieties that are sown in spring for cropping in late winter/early spring the next year. Late and early varieties extend harvesting period
Calabrese	Varieties produce green 'spears' (heads) through the late summer and autumn from an April/May sowing. Many will 'cut and come again' for continuous picking

Sow purple-sprouting broccoli in a seedbed – a small area set aside especially for raising seedlings – thinning to 7.5 cm (3 in) apart and transplanting the young seedlings in late spring/early summer when they're about 7.5 cm (3 in) tall. They need quite a bit of space in their final positions – 45 cm (18 in) between plants, a good 60 cm (2 ft) between rows. Sow calabrese seed 1 cm (½ in) deep in a seedbed or directly where they are to grow. When transplanting or thinning, allow 30–35 cm (12–14 in) between the rows and 23 cm (9 in) between plants. Always cut the central 'flower head' or spear first (to encourage side shoots) and pick further spears before the 'flowers' open up.

The main pest to watch for is the caterpillar of the cabbage white butterfly – if you see the latter around your crops, immediately inspect the underside of the leaves for signs of eggs. Remove and destroy these and, as a matter of routine, check the crop regularly, picking off any of the above-mentioned caterpillars as you find them.

Brussels Sprouts

This favourite winter vegetable has the same soil and site requirements as broccoli and is equally prone to damage by cabbage white caterpillars, so keep your eyes peeled. While they traditionally require quite a bit of space, some of the newer varieties of sprout can be grown much closer together. Most important is to pick the sprouts before they start to 'blow'.

Variety	Description
F1 hybrids	Strongly recommended, producing crowds of uniform, tightly packed sprouts that are slow to 'blow'. Early and late varieties allow extended harvesting
Ordinary	Among these are some old favourites, said by some to be unbeatable for good size and flavour. But you must be ready to pick them when they're just right

Sow an early variety in early April and transplant in May for a crop in September. For harvesting from October to March/April, sow in April and transplant in June. A selection of varieties will ensure a succession of cropping. Sow thinly in a seedbed, just 1 cm (½ in) deep in rows 15 cm (6 in) apart. Transplant when the plants are 7.5–10 cm (3–4 in) high. As for final spacing, the closer the plants are, the more sprouts you will have ready for picking at one time but the smaller they'll be. Plants further apart produce sprouts over a longer period. The distance between plants could therefore be anything from 45–75 cm (18–30 in), but it's best to stick to the wider spacing.

Cabbage

Ground preparation and soil and site requirements are the same as for broccoli.

All types are sown in a seedbed, in drills, 1 cm (½ in) deep, with some 15 cm (6 in) between rows. Sow thinly and transplant when the seedlings are about 7.5 cm (3 in) high. Spring cabbages should be

Variety	Description
Spring cabbage	Sow in late summer to provide tender young leaves in spring (spring greens) and also fully formed, though small, conical heads later on
Summer cabbage	For cabbages in August and September, sow outside in April. Early varieties can be sown under cloches in early spring for cropping in July
Winter cabbage	This term includes white cabbage and Savoy. Sow in May for harvesting from November onwards

transplanted in September/October, spaced 15 cm (6 in) apart for spring greens, 30 cm (12 in) apart for mature heads. Summer cabbages, transplanted in May/June, should be about 37 cm (15 in) apart, as should winter varieties, which are transplanted in July.

Carrot

Thanks to the many new and improved varieties, growing carrots presents no real problems these days. Choose a sunny site and go for the long-rooted varieties only if you have deep, fertile, sandy soil. To prevent damage by carrot fly, try to disturb the crop as little as possible – sow the seed thinly to reduce the need for thinning later on.

Variety	Description
Short-rooted	Some are almost round. Quick to mature and the earliest. Sow in succession for a regular supply
Medium-rooted	All-purpose varieties, sown for pulling when young and for leaving to mature for storage
Long-rooted	Generally grown as the main storing crop

The first crop can be sown under cloches in early March for pulling in June. Outside sowings, every three to four weeks from April to the end of June, will provide crops for eating from July to October and for storage. Sow thinly, 1 cm (½ in) deep, in drills 15 cm (6 in) apart. If thinning is necessary (to 5–7.5 cm/2–3 in apart), do this once the sun's gone down in the evening (when the carrot fly is less likely to be on the prowl). Afterwards, water the seedlings and make sure you dispose of the thinnings. Weed the crop by hand to avoid disturbing the plants and draw earth up round the base of the stems to prevent green-topped roots.

Cauliflower

The most difficult vegetable to grow. For successful results it's vital to dig the ground deeply in autumn, incorporating ample organic matter, and to take great care throughout the growing cycle, paying particular attention to watering – the soil must never dry out since any check to growth leads to the formation of tiny, premature heads. Winter types are suitable only for Midlands and southern gardens.

Variety	Description
Summer	Early and late varieties, mostly quite compact, allow crops from June to the end of August
Autumn	Various large or compact (Australian) varieties that can be harvested from September to December
Winter	Large-headed varieties, selected for their hardiness

Sow seed very thinly, 1 cm (½ in) deep, in drills some 15 cm (6 in) apart. Thin to 7.5 cm (3 in) and transplant when 13–15 cm (5–6 in) high. Take special care to keep the ground moist and cause as little root disturbance as possible (keep plenty of soil around the seedlings' roots when lifting). Sow summer varieties outdoors in a seedbed in April and transplant in early June. Sow autumn and winter types in early May, transplanting in July. Space plants 60 cm (2 ft) apart, compact varieties slightly closer.

Courgette

A far more fashionable vegetable these days than the good old marrow, although this is essentially what a courgette is – a marrow cut before it reaches maturity. However, varieties have been developed specifically for the production of courgettes (or zucchini). They are very prolific, so you'll want only a few plants. Choose a sunny site and dig in plenty of organic matter where the plants are to grow. Crops are usually trouble-free, although slugs may cause damage – scatter slug pellets around the plants or use traps (plastic beakers filled with beer and sunk into the ground). Harvest regularly to ensure a succession of fruits right through the season.

Variety	Description
Green	The most usual colour. Several varieties, some earlier than others. Produce fruits in profusion as long as they are harvested regularly
Gold	Golden-coloured varieties are no different in flavour but make a welcome contribution to the look of a dish

SOWING COURGETTES AND CUCUMBERS

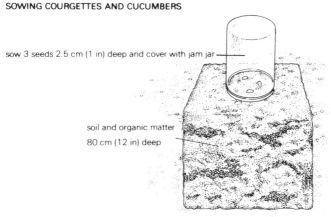

sow 3 seeds 2.5 cm (1 in) deep and cover with jam jar

soil and organic matter
80 cm (12 in) deep

prepare 30 cm (12 in) square planting pockets

The seed needs to be sown in warm soil, so wait until the end of May/early June and in colder areas use cloches to be on the safe side. Plants can be started indoors in peat pots (the pot itself is later planted) for transplanting in June. Because courgettes dislike any root disturbance (hence the use of peat pots), sow seed outside in prepared planting pockets, 60 cm (2 ft) apart, where the plants are to grow. These should be 30 cm (12 in) square and 30 cm (12 in) deep and be filled with organic matter/compost and soil. Sow three seeds, 2.5 cm (1 in) deep and 2.5 cm (1 in) or so apart, in each. Cover the seeds with a cloche or jam jar to encourage germination. Thin the seeds to the strongest seedling. It is very important to keep the ground constantly moist.

Cucumber

The arrival of F1 hybrids and all-female varieties has revolutionised the growing of outdoor cucumbers – now you can look forward to crops every bit as good as those grown in a greenhouse. Their basic requirements are the same as for courgettes and, in turn, they demand identical ground preparation and plant-raising techniques. Seed can be sown at the same time, either under cover or outside, to provide a harvest from about the end of July through to around mid-September.

Variety	Description
Ridge	These are the traditional outdoor 'cues' – short and stout with lumpy skins. F1 varieties are very hardy, more attractive (and longer) and resistant to disease. There are dwarf types, too, that need very little space and will even grow in pots
All-female	Unlike ridge types, these don't need to be fertilised (hence no male flowers). The cucumbers are also virtually seedless
Japanese	These have the longest fruits and smoothest skins, rivalling greenhouse cucumbers

Sow seed (as for courgettes) in planting pockets 45 cm (18 in) apart. To help preserve moisture in the soil and keep it warm, lay black polythene over the surrounding ground – this will also keep the weeds down and stop the fruits getting soiled. Climbing varieties will need supporting on a tripod of canes.

Leek

This often underrated winter vegetable is not at all demanding, although it is necessary to have well dug, free-draining soil and to take care with transplanting and watering. Leeks are generally untroubled by pests and diseases. There isn't an overwhelming range of varieties and so it's easy enough to find ones that will allow cropping from the end of the year through to April – all from outside sowings in March/April.

Sow the seed thinly in a seedbed, 1 cm (½ in) deep, in drills 15 cm (6 in) apart. Transplant when they are about 7.5–15 cm (3–6 in) high – usually in May or June. Water the prepared bed and the seedbed the day before. Then, on the day, prepare the planting holes, 23 cm (9 in) apart and 15 cm (6 in) deep, using a dibber, before carefully lifting the seedlings. Each of these is lowered into a hole, which is then filled up with water – this holds them firm, so don't fill with earth! As the plants develop, draw up earth around the stems, little by little, to keep them nice and white. Never pull leeks out of the ground – ease them out gently with a fork – and don't leave them to get too big, otherwise the flavour will suffer.

Lettuce

There are four main types of lettuce – cos, butterhead (or 'cabbage'), crisphead (a 'cabbage' type) and leaf (or loose-leaf) – all of which offer a good selection of varieties. The cos lettuce is slightly trickier to grow and the leaf types don't form hearts. The butterhead and crisphead varieties are more popular and generally more reliable. Summer lettuce, which is best sown in small quantities in succession, needs a reasonably sunny site.

Variety	Description
Butterhead	Most varieties are fairly easy-going and are quick to mature. A few can be sown in late summer for harvesting the following spring or raised under cloches for an early crop. Most are summer varieties for growing in succession
Crisphead	Some are wonderfully frilly, others are white-hearted Iceberg types. Most are summer varieties, but one or two can be grown for an autumn crop

For outside sowings of summer and autumn lettuce, sow seed thinly, 1 cm (½ in) deep, in drills 15–23 cm (6–9 in) apart depending on variety. Thin to 7.5 cm (3 in) and then again, according to the seed packet instructions. Start sowings outside in late March (or a bit earlier under cloches) and continue through to mid-July. You can then be cropping until about mid-October. For a lettuce crop up until Christmas, sow seed of a suitable variety in August, covering with cloches in September (close up the ends of the cloches).

Onion

It's possible to raise both bulb onions and shallots from sets (specially grown immature bulbs) and from seed. Sets are best if your soil is difficult to work or poor or if you live in a particularly cold part of the country.

Variety	Description
Bulb types	Various shapes, sizes and skin colours. Sowing in spring for an August/September crop. Thinnings can be used for salads and the harvested bulbs will store until the following year
Salad types	Several varieties, producing slender, mild 'spring' onions with white skins. Quick-growing, they can be harvested from March to October

The ground for onions should have been well dug in autumn. It should be nice and firm and also fairly sunny so that the onions will ripen. Sow the seed thinly in March/April where the plants are to

MAKING AN ONION ROPE

1 double up a long piece of string and loop round first onion

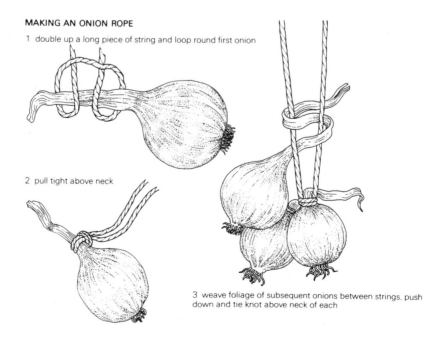

2 pull tight above neck

3 weave foliage of subsequent onions between strings, push down and tie knot above neck of each

grow, 1 cm (½ in) deep, in drills 23 cm (9 in) apart. Thin to 7.5 cm (3 in) apart. Sets can be planted in 2.5 cm (1 in) deep drills 23 cm (9 in) apart in March or April, with 7.5 cm (3 in) between each small bulb.

Salad onions can be sown in succession from March to July for pulling from June to October – sow in August for crops from March to May of the following year.

The foliage of bulb types will topple over when the onions are mature. Leave them for a couple of weeks and then gently prise the bulbs out of the ground. If it's fine and sunny, leave them lying on the ground to dry – otherwise, find room to dry them indoors. This may take several weeks, after which they can be strung up in nets or old nylon tights/stockings or tied in traditional ropes for storage in a cool, frost-free place.

Parsnip

The great thing about this vegetable is that it needs minimal attention and can be harvested as required – it will be ready and waiting whenever you want to throw a few in with the Sunday roast. There are relatively few varieties, some long-rooted, others fairly stumpy. The latter tend to be easier, being less demanding in terms of soil conditions and more practical when it comes to peeling and cooking. Generally, the same ground preparation and site is required as for other root crops (see 'Beetroot', page 90).

In March sow groups of three seeds, 1 cm (½ in) deep and 15 cm (6 in) apart, in drills – keep the rows 30 cm (12 in) apart. Thin to the strongest seedling at each sowing position (or 'station', as it is often called). Weed carefully, without touching or disturbing the tops (crowns) of the roots, and water when the weather is dry. In cold areas lift the roots (they'll be ready by about the end of October) and store. Otherwise, simply dig them up when needed.

Radish

Perhaps the easiest vegetable of all and, provided that you like them, one of the most welcome. There are a few winter varieties, which are much bigger and stronger, but as the summer types are the ones we all know (and love?), we'll deal only with these. Most are red or red/white and either globular or cylindrical in shape. Their basic requirements and cultivation are the same, whatever the variety.

You can start sowing under cloches as early as the end of January, giving you crops from the beginning of April. Sow outside from mid-March to early June, every few weeks, to have a continuous supply from May to the end of August. Space-sow the seed (it's a reasonable size), 1 cm (½ in) deep in drills 15 cm (6 in) apart. Thinning won't be necessary. Radishes take around three to six weeks to mature depending upon their growing conditions.

Spinach

There are two types of real spinach, one grown for picking in summer, the other for winter cropping. Spinach beet belongs to the beetroot family and is an excellent alternative on poor or dry soil since it won't run to seed. For pleasantly flavoured leaves, it's essential to have soil rich in organic matter. While summer varieties will want a slightly shaded site (grow them between taller-growing vegetables), winter types should get as much sun as possible. Choose varieties that are resistant to bolting (running to seed) and to the disease 'downy mildew' (spinach is quite susceptible) and be prepared to water copiously whenever there's a dry spell. Spinach will not tolerate long, dry spells.

Variety	Description
Summer	As long as the summer isn't too hot and dry, these varieties are quick to mature and allow picking from June right through to October
Winter	Use these for picking from October to March/April, but make sure that you cook only tender, young leaves
Spinach beet	Easier to grow than spinach with almost as good a flavour

Sow summer types and spinach beet in succession from mid-March through to the end of May in drills where the plants are to grow. The seed must be sown thinly, 2.5 cm (1 in) deep, in rows 30 cm (12 in) apart. Thin to 7.5 cm (3 in) apart as soon as the seedlings are large enough to handle and, a few weeks later, thin to about 23 cm (9 in) apart – the leaves of these thinnings can be cooked. Sow winter varieties of the plant in August and September and protect the crop with cloches in colder parts of the country. Remember to pick the leaves regularly.

Tomato

Whether growing from seed or buying in young plants (which is often more convenient if you want just a few), double-check that the variety is suitable for growing outdoors. Tomatoes need a warm, sheltered site and soil enriched with garden compost and peat. They are also an ideal crop for raising in growing-bags, perhaps on the patio against a south-facing wall. In colder, exposed areas, grow bush types under cloches and, wherever you live, wait for mild weather before planting.

Variety	Description
Cordon type	Climbing plants with trusses forming on a single stem. Require some training and must be supported. Many different fruit sizes, forms, colours
Bush type	Sturdy bushes (some as low as 30 cm/12 in) or creeping plants needing no support/training. Good yields. Some quite hardy for colder areas/early crops. Lay plastic/straw on ground to protect fruits

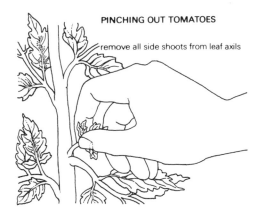

PINCHING OUT TOMATOES

remove all side shoots from leaf axils

Sow seed in trays (or three to a pot, thinning to the strongest seedling), under cover and in warmth, in late March/early April (see 'Sowing under cover', page 37). The plants will be ready for transplanting by the end of May, provided the weather is mild; this would also be the time to buy in plants. Space them 50 cm (20 in) square and support upright varieties by loosely tying the stems, at regular intervals, to stout 1.5 m (5 ft) canes. Pinch off the side shoots as they appear and pinch out the top of the main stem just above the fourth truss, once this is bearing flowers. Bush varieties need no pinching out. Keep the plants well watered, especially when the fruits are developing, and remove some of the yellowing leaves (on cordons only). When the fruits of bush types start to ripen, strip off just enough foliage to let the sun get to them. You can expect a harvest from July to October. Use of a special tomato fertiliser will improve both fruit quality and yield.

Turnip

Like the parsnip, this highly versatile vegetable is relatively undemanding, although varieties grown early in the year will need a particularly fertile soil. Being a root crop as well as a member of the brassica family means that the turnip has the same basic requirements as beetroot, carrots and so on as well as cabbages. Generally, however, turnips are trouble-free and can be enjoyed almost year-round if also grown for the tops, which can be used as 'spring greens'.

Variety	Description
Early types	Quick to mature, these are sown in succession and eaten raw or cooked when young and tender. Various shapes. Some ideal for sowing/growing under cloches
Main-crop types	These take longer to mature and are grown from one sowing for a winter supply – either stored or left in the ground. They can be sown in autumn for spring greens

Sow under cloches in February/March and in the open from late March/April at regular intervals. Main-crop varieties should be sown in late July/early August; those being grown for greens in August/September. Sow thinly in drills, 1 cm (½ in) deep, in rows 23 cm (9 in) apart or just 7.5 cm (3 in) apart for greens – thin the seedlings to 10 cm (4 in) apart. Those intended as greens needn't be thinned: the tops should be cut when about 15 cm (6 in) high and they should then grow again.

CHAPTER 8

FRUIT

The present-day small garden can accommodate a great variety of fruit thanks to a whole new range of dwarf trees and bushes. And many of these are also perfect for training against walls and fences, which means they take up still less space. So even if space is severely limited, you'll be able to grow a big enough selection of varieties to ensure a succession of harvesting over a fairly long period. In the average garden, aiming for a year-round supply of fruit is a fairly tall order, but not impossible. The table below shows how you can make maximum use of the space at your disposal.

SPACE-SAVING WAYS WITH FRUIT	
Apples	Grow dwarf bushes and cordons (main stems trained at an angle against a wall/fence/horizontal wires stretched between posts). Will tolerate almost any site. Spacing: 1.5 m (5 ft) apart; cordons 75 cm (2½ ft) apart
Pears	As for apples but need more sun
Gooseberries	Don't mind a bit of shade, so give the sunniest spot to something else. Can even be grown under standard-size fruit trees. Spacing: 1–1.2 m (3–4 ft) apart
Currants	Blackcurrants need an open, warm situation. Redcurrants can be slightly shaded and cooler but need shelter from cold winds. Spacing: 1.2 m (4 ft) apart
Raspberries	Need sun, so plant in rows running north/south. Few problems with frost. Spacing: 45 cm (18 in) apart
Strawberries	These can be planted in rows between bush fruits or in borders below wall-trained plants. And they can grow in tubs, of course. Spacing: 30 cm (1 ft)

The development of the dwarf fruit bushes, together with a much less complicated approach to pruning and training methods, has made the management of fruit easier than ever before. Many of the varieties are much improved, too, with increased resistance to frost damage and diseases. Simply give them a good start in life, with their roots in a well-dug, fertile soil, and they'll reward you for many years.

Buying the Plants

Container-grown fruit trees and bushes can be planted at any time of year, but those that are bare-rooted (lifted from open ground in the nursery) must be planted during the winter months when the plants are dormant. November, in fact, is the traditional time for fruit planting – because the ground isn't too cold or frozen – but if the weather is mild, it can be carried out until the end of February. Bare-rooted types need to be planted immediately you get them home, which means the proposed site will have to be prepared in advance. Finally, always buy from a reputable source and go only for named varieties of plants.

Choosing Varieties

For each of the popular fruits covered in this chapter, there is a shortlist of recommended varieties, chosen primarily for their good fruit quality, reliability and ease of management. In the case of bush fruits, such as gooseberries and blackcurrants, the varieties have also been selected for their naturally compact habit of growth. However, it is worth explaining here that with varieties of tree fruits – such as apples and pears – it is mainly the rootstock that dictates the tree's ultimate size and vigour. The same variety, therefore, can grow into a full-size tree on one rootstock but remain a dwarf bush on another. That's why it's important to check that your chosen variety is being offered on an appropriate rootstock – those used for dwarf plants put all their energy into producing fruit rather than wood and are therefore the ideal choice when space in the garden is fairly limited. For high-yielding dwarf bushes and cordons choose apple varieties on an M27 or M9 rootstock and pear varieties on a Quince C rootstock.

Another factor to consider when choosing varieties of apples and pears is pollination. Some are self-fertile but these tend not to be particularly high-yielding or reliable. That's why the best plan, generally, is to go for a minimum of two different varieties which are compatible and will therefore pollinate each other (see the recommendations). Alternatively, you could choose a single 'family' tree, which has two or more compatible varieties all growing on the same rootstock. Bear in mind, however, that the more neighbours you have with an apple or pear tree in their garden, the less likely it is that you will experience any real problems with pollination.

Apples

Although apples are the 'tough guys' of the fruit world, it would be wise to choose a frost-resistant variety if your garden is prone to prolonged, hard frosts. For good-sized, juicy fruit, the ground needs to hold as much moisture as possible, so be generous with the organic matter or garden compost when digging the planting site.

Varieties	Harvesting	Description
'Discovery'	Aug/Sept	Early-season dessert apple with very attractive pale green/flushed red skin. Crisp and juicy flesh. Will store better than many other earlies, but this is not really recommended
'James Grieve'	Sept/Oct	A favourite eater that continues to prove its worth. Easy to manage, very reliable and a good pollinator. Fruit is strongly flavoured with green/red-streaked skins. Storage: three to four weeks
'Spartan'	Nov/Jan	Striking dark red dessert apple with pleasantly flavoured, crisp flesh. Especially hardy, so is ideal for northern parts of the country
'Lane's Prince Albert'	Nov/Mar	A good cooker for a small garden with reliable crops of good-sized fruits. A late keeper that will do well in colder areas

Note: all the above will pollinate each other. The harvesting period is for an average climate as found in, say, southern areas of Britain

Planting

Apples, like all fruit, should be planted early – in November, say – so that they can get settled in before any hard frosts. If the ground is unexpectedly frozen (or waterlogged) when you are due to plant, store the young trees in a frost-free place, with the roots still wrapped, until conditions improve. Don't allow the roots to dry out.

As you will be buying either one-year-old (maiden) or, at most, two-year-old trees, the root systems won't need huge planting holes – generally, 30 cm (12 in) deep by 45 cm (18 in) square will be quite sufficient. For a row of cordon trees, it is easier to dig out a continuous trench, positioned so that the main stems will be at least 23 cm (9 in) away from the fence or wall. Put some extra organic matter into the

PLANTING CONTAINER-GROWN BARE-ROOTED FRUIT

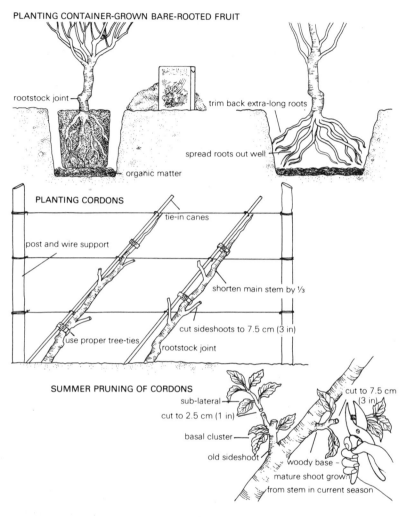

rootstock joint

trim back extra-long roots

spread roots out well

organic matter

PLANTING CORDONS

tie-in canes

post and wire support

shorten main stem by ⅓

cut sideshoots to 7.5 cm (3 in)

use proper tree-ties

rootstock joint

SUMMER PRUNING OF CORDONS

sub-lateral

cut to 7.5 cm (3 in)

cut to 2.5 cm (1 in)

basal cluster

old sideshoot

woody base

mature shoot grown from stem in current season

bottom of the planting holes (or along the trench), plus a liberal sprinkling of a fertiliser such as bonemeal.

The roots of the trees should be thoroughly moist, so soak them in water for a couple of hours prior to planting – the same goes for container-grown plants, which should be well watered. All trees on dwarfing rootstocks must be staked. Cordons are trained at a 45 degree angle against a post-and-wire support.

With container-grown plants, you simply tap-out the root-ball from the pot and position it centrally and squarely in the prepared hole, making sure that the joint between the rootstock and the variety is well above soil level. You'll easily recognise it as a distinct kink in the stem. With bare-rooted trees, spread out the roots within the hole/trench and trim back the odd one that is too long, using a pair of secateurs – don't try to bend them in to fit! Fill in around the roots with soil, firming it down with your foot as you go (to get rid of air pockets) and making sure that the joint between rootstock and variety is well above the soil level. Secure the stem to the stake, using a proprietary tree-tie to avoid damaging the bark.

All that remains for you to do with bush types is to shorten all the branches by one third, which simply involves cutting them back with a sharp pair of secateurs.

Growing cordons
Cordons should be pruned immediately after planting. Cut back any side shoots to about 7.5 cm (3 in). As with bush fruits, cut back the main stem by about a third; the only other pruning required should be carried out in summer.

PRUNING REQUIREMENTS	
Early August	**Cordons:** Cut back mature shoots (with a woody base) that have grown from the main stem in the current season to 7.5 cm (2 in). Cut back growth (sub-laterals) from existing/old side shoots to 2.5 cm (1 in) – just above the cluster of leaves at the base
	Bushes: Treat each branch as if it were the main stem of a cordon and prune as above

Aftercare
All fruit trees will benefit from a little pampering once the worst of the winter is over and before the growing season gets into full swing. In February apply a rose fertiliser to the ground and follow this with a good, thick layer of your own garden compost or some well-rotted manure. Water is especially critical in the first year, so keep the ground nice and moist during dry spells and reduce competition for moisture by weeding on a regular basis. If late frosts are a problem when the trees are in blossom, try to protect them at night by draping them with sacking or some similar material.

Pests and diseases
There are few plants in the garden that aren't attractive to greenfly and tree fruits are no exception. If you see the tell-tale sign of young

leaves and shoots starting to curl up, spray immediately with an appropriate proprietary insecticide. Other causes for concern are dealt with in the table below:

Problem	Signs	Treatment
Scab	Brown blistering on shoots, leaves and fruits	Spray with protective fungicide
Codling moth	Little white grubs burrow into fruits, leaving dirty holes on skin	Spray with a combined systemic/contact proprietary insecticide for fruit during June and July

Pears

Apart from the fact that pears require a warm, sunny position if they are to mature and ripen properly, they can be treated almost exactly as for apples. You can therefore refer to 'Apples' (above) for information on ground preparation, planting, training/pruning and general aftercare/control of pests and diseases. The advice given regarding choice of varieties and buying of plants also applies to pears.

Varieties	Harvesting	Description
'Williams'	Sept	Heavy, early crops of golden fruits with soft, juicy flesh. Ideal all-rounder, which bottles well. Not self-fertile. Pick before fully ripe
'Conference'	Oct/Nov	Reliable crops of olive-green/russet-skinned fruits with sweet, juicy flesh. Very hardy – good for colder parts of the country. Stores well
'Doyenné du Comice'	Nov/Dec	Yellowish green/flushed red skins and the best-flavoured flesh. Needs a sheltered site and takes a fairly long time to ripen fully

Note: Choose two of the above so that they will pollinate each other

Harvesting and storage

Pears have a rather more delicate constitution than apples so are not generally as successful. Harvest them before they get too ripe and fall off the tree. To be on the safe side, pick when still quite firm and finish ripening indoors. Store in a warm, dry, dark place where you can maintain a temperature of around 10°C (50°F).

Gooseberries

The distinctive flavour and texture of the gooseberry is not to everyone's taste, which is a great shame since it is the most undemanding of soft fruits and will usually thrive without your paying it the least bit of attention. Perhaps that explains why a 'gooseberry' is also the unfortunate third person in the 'two's company, three's a crowd' situation! Certainly, the gooseberry fruit is both tough and resilient, tolerating any amount of frost and exposure to cold winds. It will also grow happily in semi-shade.

The most usual harvesting period for gooseberries is June/July, although some can be picked earlier (when still green) for cooking and others can be picked later because they keep their fruits on the bush for slightly longer – for this reason they are categorised as early, mid-season and late varieties. None could be said to have a compact habit but the following varieties number among the less vigorous, each forming a fairly manageable, spreading bush.

Varieties	Type	Description
'Invicta'	Mid-season	Large, greenish-white berries with a smooth skin. Excellent for freezing/jam-making or eating raw. Fruit will have a good size/flavour early in the season
'Leveller'	Late	Very large, yellowish berries with smooth skin. Pick when green for freezing or wait until ripe for eating off the bush. Very sweet fruit – one of the best
'Whinham's Industry'	Late	Large, hairy, dark red fruits – ideal for cooking/bottling and, later on, for eating raw. Good flavour. Doesn't mind heavy soil

Planting

Most gooseberries do best in a light, free-draining soil. Prepare the ground well, therefore, incorporating enough organic matter to retain moisture in summer. The time to plant is November, before the frosts arrive, but if the ground is particularly heavy, wait until early March. Make sure that the site is cleared of weeds because getting rid of these once the bush is established may prove a thorny problem! Prepare the planting holes as described for apples (page 105), allowing 1.2–1.5 m (4–5 ft) between bushes and a distance of some 60 cm (2 ft) from any adjacent plants or permanent features.

Pruning

Bushes can be allowed to develop naturally for the first few years, after which pruning will simply involve the removal of old, unproductive wood and any branches that have become over-crowded. If you want to encourage a more upright habit, cut the lower, drooping branches back by half, to a bud facing upwards. To keep bushes low and open in the middle, cut back the upper branches to a bud facing outwards. All such work should be carried out in winter.

Aftercare

As with all soft fruits, sufficient moisture in the soil is vital if the fruits are to swell and ripen. In dry spells – and especially once the fruits have formed – water copiously, preferably in the evening. Watering should continue on a regular basis until the fruit is ripe.

Pests and diseases

Generally, gooseberries are most troubled by just one pest and one disease, both of which are fortunately fairly easy to control:

Problem	Signs	Treatment
Gooseberry sawfly	Caterpillars (brown or yellow/ black spots) appear from May onwards, stripping the leaves	Must be controlled or fruit size will suffer. Pick off caterpillars; dust plant with derris
American gooseberry mildew	White powder on leaves; felt-like brown mould on fruit	Cut out affected shoots/ branches. Spray with systemic fungicide for fruit, before flowering and after fruit set

Strawberries

Just as the gooseberry is a prime example of the less popular fruits always being the easiest to please, so the strawberry's immense popularity automatically makes it one of the more difficult characters in the fruit kingdom! Nevertheless, the appearance of some quite hardy varieties, together with the use of cloches for protection from the elements, means that they can be enjoyed fresh from the garden.

Buying plants

If you buy plants by mail order, these will usually be despatched in

Varieties	Harvesting	Description
'Elsanta'	Jun/Jul	Not too fussy over soil conditions and resistant to frost/drought. Reliable cropping with high yields – can be grown under cloches
'Aromel'	Sept/Oct	Invaluable for its late harvesting season, especially if later crops are grown under cloches. Large, tasty berries. Also good for tubs
'Honeyoe'	Early Jun	A new variety producing good crops of well-flavoured fruit

August/September, in plenty of time to give you a first crop by June of the next year – indeed, strawberries are the quickest of all fruits to come into bearing. To ensure freedom from disease, always buy from a specialist supplier.

Planting

Give strawberries a sunny site and incorporate plenty of organic matter in order to retain moisture in the soil. Nearer planting time apply a light dressing of rose fertiliser and remove any large bits of organic matter that haven't broken down – especially those near or on the soil surface. Use a trowel to dig out shallow planting holes, 30 cm (12 in) apart, that will accommodate the spreading roots and just lightly cover with soil, making sure that the 'crown' of each plant (where the leaves join the roots) is exactly at soil level. Firm in the plants and water well.

PLANTING STRAWBERRIES

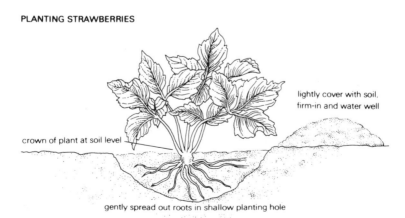

lightly cover with soil, firm-in and water well

crown of plant at soil level

gently spread out roots in shallow planting hole

Aftercare

Strawberries planted in the open in spring will be starting to flower by about mid-May. This is the time to lay straw on the ground around each plant (commonly called mulching) in order to keep the developing fruits clean and the soil warm and moist. Black polythene works equally well. It will still be necessary to water during dry spells, however, and especially when the fruits are swelling and ripening. Given half a chance, of course, the birds will be swiping your strawberries long before you have a chance to sample them, so protect them with netting.

Plants being raised under cloches in spring should be well ventilated and, on warm days, left uncovered until early evening to let the bees pollinate them. Lightly mist the flowers with water to encourage pollination and make sure that the ground under the cloches is kept nice and moist. Varieties that are still producing fruits in late summer/autumn can be protected with cloches to aid ripening and protect the fruits from the elements.

Strawberries tend to suffer from a shortage of potassium in the soil. To rectify this, feed the plants in late January/early February each year with rose fertiliser applied at a rate of 25 g per sq m (1 oz per sq yd).

Pests and diseases

Avoid potential problems by growing varieties that are resistant or less susceptible to virus diseases, moulds and mildews. As for pests, keep a look out for greenfly, spraying the plants with a suitable insecticide if seen, and also slugs, which can be removed by hand and disposed of or, alternatively, treated with slug bait.

Blackcurrants and Redcurrants

Cold winds and frosts spell disaster for blackcurrants, so give them a warm, sheltered site but not one that is overshadowed. Redcurrants don't mind being slightly shaded and aren't bothered by frosts – however, they are even less tolerant of cold winds than blackcurrants. For good-sized, juicy blackcurrants, the soil must be quite heavy and rich in organic matter, which will not only make it fertile and water-retentive but will also help to raise the nutrient level (to encourage new wood to form for fruit production).

Normally two-year-old bushes of both types of currant are offered for sale. If planted in November, redcurrants will start to crop in the

PLANTING CURRANTS

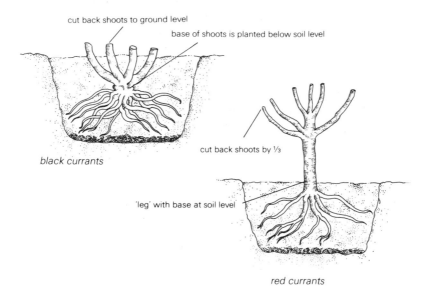

cut back shoots to ground level

base of shoots is planted below soil level

cut back shoots by ⅓

black currants

'leg' with base at soil level

red currants

following year, while blackcurrants will take two years to come into bearing. The reason for this is that while both produce fruit on old and new wood, redcurrants form fruit on the current season's shoots and blackcurrants on the previous season's. And since blackcurrants are cut hard back at planting time (leaving no old wood), it is new wood that bears the first crops.

Varieties	Harvesting	Description
'Ben Sarek'	July/Aug	A new variety making a very compact bush, so ideal for small gardens. Heavy cropper
'Ben More'	July/Aug	Probably the heaviest cropper of them all
'Red Lake'	Aug	Superb dessert-quality redcurrants on compact bush with tough constitution. Bright scarlet fruits. Good for jelly

Planting

Timing and basic preparations are the same as for apples (page 105). Plant about 1.2–1.5 m (4–5 ft) apart. Redcurrants are grown on a leg, so they're planted in the same way as apples (though without the stakes). Blackcurrants produce strong shoots from below ground, so plant them a little deeper than they grew in the nursery.

Pruning
After planting, cut all the shoots on blackcurrants hard back to ground level. Reduce the shoots of redcurrants by about a third. After that, little pruning will be required for redcurrants in the first few years (see 'Gooseberries', page 109) and none for blackcurrants in the second year. In the following years prune blackcurrants by cutting back all the wood that has fruited every autumn, to make way for new young shoots.

Aftercare
To keep the soil fertile and to help retain moisture during the summer, mulch the ground around the plants in spring with a generous layer of manure or garden compost. Currants are particularly attractive to birds, so cover the bushes with netting.

Pests and diseases
As with other soft fruits, many problems can be avoided by buying healthy, virus-free plants and choosing varieties that are lest susceptible to mildew. The main pest is greenfly.

Raspberries

By growing a combination of summer- and autumn-fruiting varieties, it's possible to enjoy this favourite fruit from June through to November. Raspberries need a sunny site and they will get the most sun by being planted in a row running north–south. Soil preparation is the same as for blackcurrants since they prefer quite heavy ground and require plenty of humus. Their requirements are also not dissimilar to those of strawberries (page 110) and they are equally vulnerable to a shortage of potassium – prior to planting, therefore, rake in rose fertiliser at a rate of 25 g per m (1 oz per yd) of row. Summer-fruiting raspberries fruit on the previous season's growth, autumn types on the current season's (see 'Aftercare' opposite).

Planting
In November dig a trench 60 cm (2 ft) wide. Mix in plenty of organic

Varieties	Harvesting	Description
'Glen Prosen'	Jun/Jul	High yields of firm fruits with a very good flavour. Long harvesting period and good all-rounder
'Malling Admiral'	Aug	Heavy crops of large, very firm berries – excellent for freezing/bottling. Resistant to mildew/virus
'Autumn Bliss'	Aug/Oct	A newish variety, said by many to be the best autumn type. Very high yields and lovely flavour

matter and refill. Plant the canes 45 cm (18 in) apart and then cut them back to within 15 cm (6 in) of the ground. Autumn-fruiting kinds will bear fruit the following year, summer types the year after next.

Aftercare

As the canes grow, provide support by tying them to horizontal wires, 45 cm (18 in) apart, stretched between posts at either end of the row. The canes should be about 10 cm (4 in) apart. Remove weak or damaged canes. Autumn varieties need no support. After fruiting the following year, cut out the old canes that have fruited and tie in new ones to the wires, again about 10 cm (4 in) apart. Cut back autumn-fruiting canes to the ground in February. Lay a mulch of peat/composted straw around the plants in late May each year in order to keep weeds down and preserve moisture in the soil.

Pests and diseases

The raspberry beetle may lay its eggs on the flowers, which means fruits get eaten by the emerging grubs – to control, dust or spray with derris at flowering and again at fruit set.

CHAPTER 9

CONTAINER GARDENING

Growing ornamental plants in containers gives you the unique opportunity to have a splash of colour or a bold display of foliage virtually wherever you want – even up in the air. And just like so many ornaments or pieces of furniture, you can move them around at will for a change of scene or mood. But perhaps even more important still is the fact that the use of tubs, troughs, wall pots, hanging baskets and windowboxes means you can then make the very most of all those plants whose individual qualities would tend to be lost if left to do battle with bolder subjects in the shrub border. Displays in containers, after all, are invariably placed near to the house – very often adorning the walls themselves – which makes them far more accessible and, in turn, subject to much closer scrutiny.

Special features, therefore, such as distinctive leaf markings, intricate flower forms and sweet-smelling scents will be appreciated to the full. And such plants will prove invaluable whatever the nature of the container and wherever it happens to be positioned – put them in wall pots perhaps to soften a stark surface, in a hanging basket to welcome visitors to your door, or in a windowbox to be seen from the kitchen sink.

But for tubs, troughs and urns that are positioned on the patio, or used to flank a path or flight of steps, there is yet another group of plants that can be used to great advantage – permanent ornamentals with a boldly sculptural form, such as yucca, phormium, clipped yew or box and the hardy palms. Stand just one of these in splendid isolation and you couldn't want for a more effective focal point.

So there's a whole variety of roles that plants in containers can perform. And their performances can run right through the year if you make full use of the various types of plants at your disposal:

Planning a Display

Even in the absence of any garden at all, just a single windowbox gives you the opportunity to grow and enjoy a great many flower and foliage subjects. But the additional challenge is to create a year-

FOR A YEAR-ROUND DISPLAY IN CONTAINERS	
Plants for spring	**Comments**
Bulbs – dwarf varieties of tulip and daffodil, plus crocus, hyacinth and grape hyacinth	Plant in autumn as for border bulbs or plant in pots and plunge in compost. Not suited to hanging baskets/wall pots
Biennials – wallflower, polyanthus, primula, pansy and forget-me-not	Ideally, plant out in autumn at the same time as bulbs
Plants for summer	**Comments**
Hardy annuals – sweet alyssum, poached egg flower, candytuft, godetia, Virginian stock and Californian poppy. Grow nasturtium and sweet pea in tubs for quick cover of walls	Seed can be sown direct but for a well-planned display it's best to have young plants for planting up. All look best when there are several to a group
Half-hardy annuals – lobelia, busy Lizzie, petunia, ageratum, snap-dragon, calceolaria, gazania, mesembryanthemum, nicotiana, salvia, dwarf French marigold, pansy, zinnia	Raise from seed under cover or buy in young plants in early May, once all risk of frost is over. Double-check habit of growth (e.g. trailing or bushy). Pay attention to spacing
Tender perennials – for foliage use coleus, spider plant and fern; for flowers use trailing and bushy forms of begonia, fuchsia and geranium. In windowboxes use dwarf dahlia	Don't plant these out until you're sure the weather will stay mild. At end of summer, remove them for overwintering somewhere cool, light and frost-free. Lift and store tubers
Plants for autumn/winter	**Comments**
Permanent evergreen subjects like ivy (good in baskets), euonymus, winter heather, dwarf conifer, spotted laurel (all in tubs), sedum and sempervivum (windowboxes)	If left permanently planted, space around them can be used for fill-in seasonal plants. Specimen shrubs need a good-sized container and a well-drained yet water-retentive compost
For flower colour – bulbs such as winter aconite and snowdrop; also winter-flowering pansy	If grown in small pots, these can be plunged into the compost for a temporary show among evergreens

round display with a special character of its own and that means paying as much attention to the selection and arrangement of plants as you would for any garden border. Where several subjects are planted in one container – as they are certain to be in a windowbox – the aim should be to achieve interesting contrasts of texture and form and effective colour combinations. In summer the silver foliage of senecio is a perfect foil for the vibrant pinks and reds of petunias, for example, while the strappy, arching leaves of the spider plant looks superb rising from soft clouds of lobelia. In winter a drift of snowdrops could appear among the heathers and, come spring, sizzling red tulips could rise above a carpet of deep violet pansies.

Seasonal changes such as this can be achieved very easily if you have just a few permanently planted subjects – the evergreen foliage types, for example – and add temporary colour to the display by plunging pots of annuals or bulbs into the compost in between. Then you can simply lift them out when the show is over and replace with something else. This wouldn't work, of course, with hanging baskets, which would have to be planted up from scratch at the start of each season, but there's no reason why the use of these containers should be confined to the summer months alone.

Another consideration is the positioning of containers for an effective display. Of course, windowboxes are intended for windowsills, but they can also be attached to house walls by means of brackets, which means they can be used to advantage anywhere you like. The same goes for hanging baskets and also wall pots which are especially valuable for camouflaging eyesores such as drainpipes and for brightening up unattractive surfaces. The placing of tubs and planters on the patio calls for a little more imagination and creativity. While a substantial container can be set in splendid isolation, it's more successful to have small and medium-sized ones arranged in groups so that the various plants can complement each other and together form a more natural-looking display. The opposite extreme would be that all-too-common arrangement of identical urns symmetrically spaced around the edge of the patio, which simply tells you in no uncertain terms where the patio ends and the garden begins. This is the last thing you want, so aim instead simply to soften a corner here or an edge there and let the patio drift into the garden.

Choosing Containers

Life is made a whole lot easier by the fact that containers are available to suit every imaginable plant, whatever its habit of growth. For trailers there are wall pots, towers of stackable pots and pots on pedestals – not to mention the hanging basket. For diminutive rock plants there are shallow troughs, trays and even old sinks, while for group plantings and specimen shrubs there are stately wooden tubs, rustic half-barrels, terracotta urns and huge concrete bowls. The windowbox, in fact, is about the only type of container that can be relied on to remain more or less unchanged – simply because it is designed to fit on a ledge in front of a window – and its basic proportions (depth and width from front to back) are normally sufficiently generous to accommodate a collection of medium-sized subjects.

Selecting a container of the right shape and style for the plants you want to grow should therefore be your first priority. Equally important, though, is the material from which it is made. For while containers used only during the summer months could perhaps be safely stored away for winter, those required for permanent displays will have to brave the elements. The pros and cons of the various options are set out in the table below to help you avoid making a bad buy.

Type of material	Pros	Cons
Stone (including reconstituted)	Durable, weathers well, attractive, many designs	Fairly expensive and very difficult to move about
Terracotta	Durable if guaranteed frost-proof. Decorative designs – good colour	Good ones are expensive – cheap ones will crack in time. Compost dries out quickly in all clay pots
Glazed ceramic	Perfect for the oriental-style garden. Durable if guaranteed frost-proof	Can be extremely expensive – cheap ones can't be left outside in winter and you may not want to risk expensive ones!
Plastics	Quality plastics are extremely long-lasting and weather-resistant. Also relatively cheap	Very cheap ones will 'bio-degrade' after a few years if left outside but are useful for summer displays
Wood	Durable if the wood is specially treated with preservative or painted inside and out	Quality timber tubs are very expensive. Cheap barrels are durable and attractive in a more rustic setting
Concrete	Durable, cheaper than stone and will weather in time to look mellow	Heavy and cumbersome to move around. Can look too stark, modern or municipal in older gardens

It really is imperative that all containers used for outdoor displays have drainage holes. Those designed for the job, of course, should have adequate provision for drainage (in plastic windowboxes, for example, the holes are marked and you have to puncture them), but

PLANTING A WINDOWBOX
permanently planted evergreens

plants in plunged pots

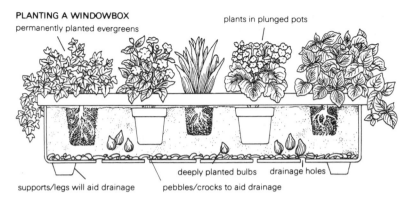

supports/legs will aid drainage

deeply planted bulbs   drainage holes

pebbles/crocks to aid drainage

if you decide to make use of a somewhat less conventional container – such as an old wheelbarrow, water butt or coal scuttle – you must attend to this yourself. Most materials can be drilled fairly easily. You must also treat all second-hand timber containers with a 'plant-safe' preservative and line the inner surface, be it metal or wood, with polythene to avoid the risk of rotting.

There's no real rule of thumb when it comes to the size of container needed for a particular display of plants – it's generally a matter of common sense, giving due regard to the spacing required by individual subjects and their ultimate height/spread. And it makes no odds either whether you choose a container to suit a plant or vice versa, just as long as they complement each other and are in proportion – that is, neither too top-heavy nor ridiculously fat-bottomed.

Types of Compost

The one thing that definitely should not find its way into your containers is the garden soil from your borders. For when plants have their roots unnaturally confined within pots, it becomes particularly essential that they are given the very best growing medium – namely, one that is free of pests/diseases and weed seeds and contains an adequate supply of nutrients, in the right proportion, to sustain healthy growth. The only way to guarantee this is to buy in supplies of specially prepared, pre-bagged compost, of the type you would use for your houseplants (see Chapter 11).

There are two basic types, one of which is soil-based, the other peat-based (or soilless). The latter has a light, open texture and is pleasant to handle but tends to dry out more quickly.

Both types, in fact, can be used to great advantage. The light texture of a peat-based compost means that young plants can root into it really quickly. It's therefore ideal for fast-growing subject like annuals, tender perennials and bulbs that are going to be only temporary residents. Where ornamentals are being given a permanent home in a container, however, the extra fertility in soil-based types will allow them to develop normally and remain undisturbed for several years. Incidentally, you can also buy pre-packed acid (ericaceous) compost for such plants as rhododendrons and azaleas, both of which are ideal subjects for tubs, though you may have to water with rainwater or acidify your tap water with a few old tea-bags.

How to Plant

Planting directly into tubs, troughs and windowboxes is exactly the same as for borders, except that annuals and so forth will usually be spaced much closer together in order to create the necessary impact. Make sure that the plants you buy are sturdy, showing every sign of glowing health, and take special care not to damage the root-balls when inserting them in their planting holes. Bulbs, too, are particularly vulnerable, so always plant these either right at the bottom of the container to grow through the other plants or put them in after the other plants have gone in. Before actually planting, you can experiment with different arrangements and find out which one works most effectively by simply positioning the plants, still in their pots, on the surface of the compost.

Hanging baskets require a quite different approach – unless, that is, the containers are little more than hanging bowls with solid sides, in which case the plants will simply trail down over the edges. The traditional hanging basket, of course, is a wire-mesh bowl that becomes completely smothered with plants growing from both the sides and the top. If it is done well, the effect can be breath-taking and it isn't as tricky as you might imagine.

You'll need a wire basket, a bag of sphagnum moss, some compost and a selection of both trailing and more compact flowering and foliage plants. Start by lining the basket with a good layer of the damp moss and then fill just the base with some compost. The root-balls of the 'lower layer' of plants can now be inserted around the sides, just above the compost level. Fill in around these with more compost, gently firming the plants in, and then plant a second 'layer', again filling in with compost. The top could be planted with, say, a specimen

PLANTING A HANGING BASKET

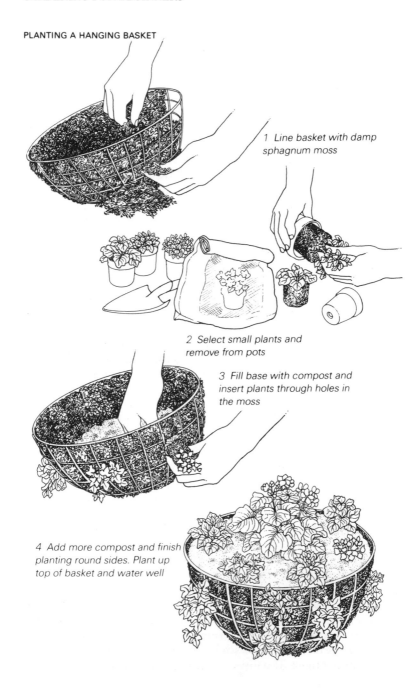

1 Line basket with damp sphagnum moss

2 Select small plants and remove from pots

3 Fill base with compost and insert plants through holes in the moss

4 Add more compost and finish planting round sides. Plant up top of basket and water well

geranium surrounded by petunias, salvias, lobelia or French marigolds with a few smaller trailing subjects to hang over the edges. Once completed, the whole basket should be really well watered.

Aftercare

Watering is critical when growing plants in containers, for the relatively small amount of compost is unable to retain moisture for very long. Added to that, containers that can 'breathe', such as clay pots and hanging baskets, are dried out by the effect of the air around them. In summer, then, watering will usually be necessary at least once a day, perhaps twice. And the only foolproof way to check whether water is needed or not is to make a 'finger test' of the compost, ensuring that you poke down a good few centimetres. Always water copiously – until you see the water beginning to trickle from the drainage hole – and preferably in the evening. Hanging baskets will certainly keep you on your toes, and literally so if you don't have a lance-type spray attachment on your hose or a pulley device on the basket so that it can be lowered to a convenient height. Come winter, permanent ornamentals can usually be left to their own devices, although it's a good idea to prevent them getting waterlogged by supporting the containers on bricks so that the drainage holes are clear of the ground.

Feeding of all the plants will be necessary when they are actively growing – bulbs in spring, for example, and annuals, tender perennials and permanent ornamentals (these to a lesser extent) in summer. Liquid fertiliser applied once a week when watering is the easiest method, although hanging baskets could need more. Use a liquid fertiliser specially made for flowers or, if you have it to hand, a tomato feed. It is possible to buy solid stick and granular fertilisers that are slow-release types and, once placed in the compost, will last for several months – a good idea for the absent-minded!

Apart from watering and feeding, routine care will consist simply of keeping your plant displays neat and tidy by dead-heading flowers as soon as they fade – this will also encourage them to flower more profusely – and trimming back/supporting any really straggly or over-vigorous growth. By late summer, tender perennials will need to be removed for overwintering somewhere cool but frost-free indoors and slightly tender permanent ornamentals should be moved, if possible, to a more sheltered position. Alternatively, take steps to protect them by wrapping the pots with sacking.

Top Ten Tips

1 Do make use of the full range of plants at your disposal, such as spring bulbs and biennials, annuals and tender perennials and specimen trees and shrubs. And don't forget the less conventional subjects such as dwarf fruit trees, roses, strawberries and herbs – even a vegetable or two!

2 Don't be tempted to cut costs, especially when creating permanent displays, by using containers of inferior quality filled with ordinary garden soil – it will prove false economy in the long run when the plants eventually keel over and the pots fall apart!

3 Do aim to create subtle combinations of foliage and flowers, with contrasting textures and forms but not madly clashing colours.

4 Do double-check the habit of growth of plants before you buy and make sure that they are given a suitable position and container – trailers need space to hang, bushy types need room to spread.

5 Don't arrange tubs and planters on the patio in gay abandon – decide the best position for, say, a single specimen shrub as a focal point and arrange smaller containers in natural groups. Consider the various angles from which the display will be viewed.

6 Do make the most of containers – hanging baskets, wall pots, windowboxes and tubs – in key positions around the house and garden: for example, by the front and back doors, against a dreary wall, next to a gate, either side of steps or at the end of a path.

7 Do bear in mind that the larger and heavier the container, the less easily it can be moved around to ring the changes. Collections of smaller pots are often far more rewarding (and usually cheaper).

8 Don't think that a summer shower will have given your plants a good soaking – very often the compost is so covered with foliage/flowers that very little rain actually penetrates.

9 Do check on a daily basis whether plants need watering – just one hot summer's day can leave them gasping for water and looking a very sorry sight the following morning.

10 Do attend to the plants' every need – watering, feeding, dead-heading and tidying/supporting as necessary – and they'll reward you for months on end.

CHAPTER 10

WATER GARDENING

Include an ornamental pool in your garden and you will be able to offer a home to a host of highly rewarding aquatic plants and, in turn, create a tranquil oasis of light, colour and form. On warm summer days, of course, the water alone will refresh and delight the eye. But add a suitable selection of pond and waterside plants and you can look forward to a visual treat come rain or shine. You'll also attract a host of birds, insects and perhaps the odd small mammal, all of whom will pay you a visit for a drink.

These days pools can be created quickly, easily and comparatively cheaply thanks to the various purpose-designed waterproof liners now on the market. So you can forget about the hassle of hiring cement mixers and so forth and concentrate instead on those aspects of design and construction that will guarantee you a garden pond both to your liking and to that of the plants.

Water gardening is by no means a hit-or-miss affair. Indeed, you have only to flick through the catalogues from the specialist aquatic suppliers to see that it is a fairly scientific art. But don't be put off! Such companies are well aware of the first-time water gardener's needs and, to that end, the pages are crammed not only with all the

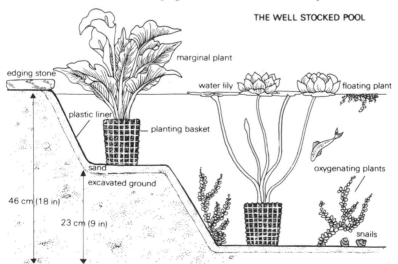

THE WELL STOCKED POOL

equipment, accessories and plants you could possibly want but also with sound advice to help you make the right decisions. Look out for their advertisements in the gardening press.

A garden pool needn't be particularly lavish or sophisticated in order to look attractive. Far more important is to ensure that it is in keeping with its surroundings and is carefully built. And just one, possibly unnecessary word of warning: if you have very small children, be aware of the dangers of a pool. The safest course is to wait until they're older before installing one in your garden.

In theory, construction work can be carried out at any time of year just as long as the ground isn't frozen or waterlogged (unless you're a glutton for punishment).

Choosing a Site

A pool needs plenty of light if the surface of the water is to display attractive reflections and the underwater environment is to remain healthy. So choose a spot that will get some sun for at least part of the day and avoid any areas that are overhung by trees or large shrubs. Bear in mind, too, that a pool is a feature to be quietly contemplated and if you can place it near to a sitting area, so much the better.

Still water usually looks most effective when it is at the lowest point in the garden, mimicking a natural landscape. If your garden is as flat as a pancake, therefore, consider using the excavated earth to build a raised bank around the edge so that the water looks lower in relation to the garden than it actually is. The area could then be planted with waterside plants (or perhaps turned into a rockery) to create a more natural transition between the pool and the surrounding lawn or patio.

Raised (or above-ground) pools are usually best sited within the patio area, where the brick retaining walls of the pool can complement the adjacent paving materials. Setting them within lawn is rarely successful – the structures are so obviously artificial that the overall effect is usually far too stark and contrived.

The only other consideration you may wish to take into account is access to mains electricity should you want to install a fountain or pool lighting. Obviously, the nearer the pool is to a power point, the less cable you will need and the easier it will be to install. Remember, though, that unless you are very competent and experienced with electrical wiring, you should always get a qualified electrician to do the necessary work.

Setting the Mood

When designing a pool, the most important decision to make is whether you want a natural-looking pool, which would be irregular in shape, or a formal one, which would be straight-edged, circular or oval.

The informal pool presents the biggest challenge to the water gardener but is invariably the most rewarding when properly executed. In order to make it appear a natural element of the garden, particular care has to be taken when it comes to choosing a site (not slap in the middle of the lawn!) and special attention must be paid to details of construction (it should not be left with the rim of the pool liner exposed for all to see!).

Scale is another consideration. Generally, 'natural' pools need to be larger than formal ones if they are to look at all convincing. You can get away with a half-barrel pool in an area of paving on the patio, but set it amidst boulders or a mass of lush vegetation and your pool will become a mere puddle. It's worth remembering, too, that when it comes to planting you'll always wish you had more space at your disposal. So, whatever style of pool you go for, try to be as generous as possible with the proportions.

How a Pool Works

Before you rush out with spade in hand to start rearranging the landscape, it would help to understand the basic workings of a garden pool and the special requirements of aquatic plants. The aim is to create a well-balanced, self-supporting environment so that the pool can be left more or less to its own devices. This is where the plants play a crucial role, for if chosen with care they will – together with a few fish and watersnails – create a natural harmony and, in turn, keep the underwater world, and your pool, looking clear and healthy.

Aquatic plants are divided into different categories, each of which have special requirements and perform specific tasks. Floating types like waterlilies, for example, provide just enough shade to prevent a build-up of algae. However, although their leaves float on the surface, their 'feet' need to be planted some distance under the water. And then there are special 'oxygenating' plants, which need to be completely submerged if they are to do their job of replacing lost oxygen in the water. The third main category is the 'marginal' plants, like bulrushes and water iris, which are planted around the edge of the pool to provide some shade and shelter and make the pool look attractive. Some of these like to be planted quite deep, while others prefer to be in shallower water.

The planting requirements of these all-important plant groups illustrate the necessity of getting the internal proportions of the pool just right. But you don't have to make it over-complicated. An overall depth of 45 cm (18 in) will suffice for waterlilies, oxygenating plants and deep marginal plants. A shelf around the edge of the pool, 23 cm (9 in) below the surface of the water, will accommodate all the 'shallow' marginal plants, or you could simply arrange for a gentle slope. Bear in mind, though, that for a pool to be adequately stocked and therefore self-supporting, the surface area shouldn't be less than around 2.3 sq m (25 sq ft).

The vast majority of aquatic plants are planted in special baskets of soil, which are then simply set in position, either on the bottom of the pool or on the marginal shelf. Incidentally, the recommended planting depth for a particular plant is measured from the surface of the water to the top of the container.

Sheet liners

The plastic or butyl-rubber liner works by moulding itself to the contours of your excavation as the pool is finally filled with water. The initial preparation, therefore, demands precise digging, measuring and levelling in order to achieve a satisfactory outline with the correct internal proportions and so forth. On the plus side, these flexible liners give you total freedom in terms of design.

There are several grades of sheet liner, the best ones being made of laminated PVC or butyl rubber, usually sold with a 'long-life' guarantee. Cheap plastic or polythene types may seem a good buy but they won't give such a neat finish and will deteriorate within a few years.

Installing a sheet liner

1 First work out the dimensions of the proposed pool so that you can calculate the size of liner required. To do this, take the widest and longest measurements and add to each the maximum depth of the pool multiplied by two – for example, a pool measuring 1.8 m × 3 m × 45 cm (6 ft × 10 ft × 18 in) will require a liner measuring 2.75 m × 4 m (9 ft × 13 ft) – and this will also allow for the necessary surplus, of about 23 cm (9 in) all around the edge. Buy the liner so that you can have it ready and waiting to finish the job.
2 Mark out with pegs the exact position and outline of the pool 15 cm (6 in) wider all round than the finished size.

BUILDING A POOL
Mark out shape with pegs and check edges are level

Move in 15 cm (6 in) from the pegs and excavate whole area to a depth of 23 cm (9 in)

Move in 23 cm (9 in) from the sides and excavate a further 23 cm (9 in)

23 cm (9 in) shelf

Remove stones, debris, etc and line with sand

Anchor liner with bricks and start to fill, using the garden hose

liner draped loosely over excavation

trim off excess liner when pool is full, leaving a 15 cm (6 in) border. (hide with soil or paving)

ease off bricks as pool fills

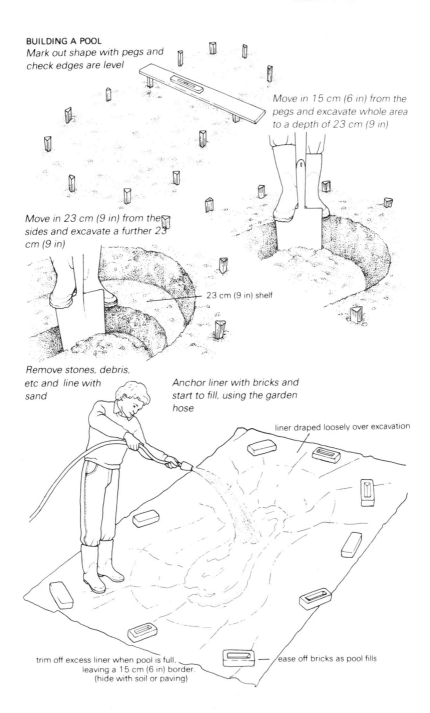

3 If you are making the pool in a lawn, remove the turf. Now level the outside edge of the pool using pegs and a spirit level. It's essential to make the edge dead level or you'll expose the liner in places, which looks very ugly.

4 If you're digging a 'stepped' pool, with shelves for marginal plants, move inwards 15 cm (6 in) all round and start by excavating the whole area to a depth of 23 cm (9 in). Now move in another 23 cm (9 in) from the sides towards the centre of the excavation. From this point inwards, you can excavate the ground to a depth of a further 23 cm (9 in), which will give you the required 45 cm (18 in) deep central area surrounded by a 23 cm (9 in) deep marginal shelf.

Alternatively, for a sloping pool, simply dig out the soil to a depth of 60 cm (2 ft), making the sides slope very gradually. The extra 15 cm (6 in) is to allow for a layer of soil for planting in the bottom.

5 With the excavations accurately completed, check over the area for any sharp stones, projecting objects, debris and so on which could tear or puncture the liner. Then, to provide an extra measure of protection, cover the whole surface, including the sides, with a 1 cm (½ in) layer of damp sand or, alternatively, a special liner that you'll be able to buy from an aquatic centre.

6 Spread the liner fairly tautly over the top of the excavated area and anchor it around the edges with bricks.

7 Fill the liner with water, gradually easing back the bricks around the edge as it moulds itself to the contours you have created. As the pool fills up, try to smooth out or neaten any creases or folds that appear round the edge.

8 Once the required level of water is reached, the surplus liner can be trimmed back to leave a neat border of 15–23 cm (6–9 in) around the sides, which can later be camouflaged with paving stones or turf. If you use paving, the slabs should be bedded on a sand-mortar mix to make sure that they are stable and, for the pool to look most effective, allowed to slightly overhang the pool edge.

With a sloping pool, refill with about 15 cm (6 in) of soil all over the liner. At first the water will naturally be brown and cloudy, but it will soon settle. At the end of the day it makes a much better job for an informal pool.

Stocking the Pool

Let the water in your new pool stand for several days before introducing the plants. And certainly don't add any fish at this stage because the plants first need to be given a chance to settle down and get established without any undue interference. This might take several weeks. And don't worry if the water looks worryingly green – it usually is in new ponds – as it will soon clear if you have a balanced selection of aquatic plants.

To this end, it really will make life a lot easier if you buy from a specialist water-garden supplier. You need some of each type of plant to create a healthy balance. A typical water-garden centre's catalogue resembles an extensive menu from a Chinese take-away! That's because it offers a choice of 'package deals', each one comprising a balanced range of plants for a particular size of pool. A typical menu for a pool measuring 2.3 sq m (25 sq ft) would be:

- One waterlily;
- Ten oxygenating plants;
- Six marginal plants;
- Three floating plants;
- Ten watersnails.

If you buy in this way – and you can do so by mail order – the plants are not specified by name. This leaves the supplier free to choose the best specimens and varieties available at the time when your order is despatched. Each plant will arrive fully named, though, and complete with planting instructions. Remember to plan for plants well in advance of the planting season to make sure that they are delivered at the appropriate time.

While mail order purchasing is the easiest way of ensuring that you get the right mix and number of plants, it does take a lot of fun out of the plant selection process. So if you want to really enjoy yourself, pay a visit to the specialist suppliers or nurseries and see the plants 'in the flesh'. That way you will get heaps of inspiration, plenty of sound advice, and just the plants you want.

Top Ten Aquatic Plants

Waterlilies (*Nymphaea*)
'Albatross': This one has impressive, large flowers with fairly narrow, pure white petals standing quite erect around the golden centre, making a striking contrast with the fresh, apple-green leaves that are

tinged purple when young. It's not too vigorous for the average pool, reaching a maximum spread of about 1.2 m.

'James Brydon': This is a must for any size of garden pool as its spread will adapt to the conditions provided. It will also thrive without a great deal of sun. Added to all that, it looks absolutely stunning with its rich pink/red cup-shaped blooms (like a peony), each some 13 cm (5 in) across, floating amidst bronzy-green foliage.

'Aurora': A superb variety, especially for smaller pools as it reaches no more than about 60 cm (2 ft) across. Most unusually, yet aptly considering its name, the flowers first appear pale yellow and then change quite rapidly through orange to dark red. What's more, the foliage is attractively mottled.

Oxygenating plants

Goldfish weed *(Elodea crispa)*: The most widely grown submerged plant, commonly seen in goldfish bowls. It has crisp, dark green foliage which floats under the surface like so many lengths of rope. A very efficient oxygenator, it is also virtually evergreen, which means that it starts earning its keep early in the year when there's the greatest risk of algae.

Marginal plants

Sweet flag *(Acorus calamus)*: A shallow marginal plant with striking grass-like foliage some 60 cm (2 ft) high or more. It will immediately make any pond look like 'the real thing'. If you can find the variety 'Variegatus', you can look forward to the foliage being streaked cream and pink. Planting depth is only a couple of inches.

Marsh marigold *(Caltha palustris)*: This one thrives best when just barely covered with water. Its glowing, golden-yellow flowers will brighten the pool edge from March to May, the whole plant reaching no more than about 30 cm (1 ft) high. Other forms include *C.p.* 'Alba', with white flowers, which grows to only 15 cm (6 in), and one that is a real yellow giant, *Caltha polypetala*, which reaches a height of up to 1 m (3 ft).

Water iris *(Iris laevigata)*: Another shallow marginal plant and, again, indispensable, but this time for its showy lavender-blue flowers in June amidst spiky, erect foliage. Like the sweet flag, there's a variegated version that's worth looking out for, and there are also varieties with white, pink or purple/white blooms.

Golden club *(Orontium aquaticum)*: A deep-water marginal – planting depth about 25–30 cm (10–12 in) – this one has an easy-going nature and silvery-green, elongated leaves that form a fairly bushy clump on the water's surface. Fanning out from these in late spring/ early summer are delicately poker-shaped, gently bobbing, yellow and white blooms.

Floating plant

Water soldier or water cactus (Stratiotes aloides): An unusual plant that won't fail to catch the eye with its pineapple-type foliage forming a striking rosette of green, red and bronze tones. In late summer there are delicate white flowers to complete the picture.

Poolside plants

Primulas: Plant these in a border beside your pool and you couldn't want for more in terms of water-garden character and colour. And they'll need virtually no attention, except for watering during dry spells. The flowering season is spring/early summer and especially worthwhile varieties include *Primula bulleyana, P. beesiana, P. florindae* and the charming little native species, *P. veris*.

CHAPTER 11

HOUSEPLANTS

Not so many decades ago, in homes across the country, a houseplant was a single aspidistra that did little more than gather dust in the gloom of a dining room or hall. Fortunately, those days are long gone. Plants around the home are now part and parcel of interior design, ranking alongside furnishings and fabrics for their ability to set a certain style. But that's not all they have to offer. Indoor gardening also enables you to enjoy the special qualities of those plants that would be hard pressed to survive out in the open. And, in turn, you can rise to the challenge of meeting the plants special requirements.

The conditions found in the average home will support a whole range of plants that are native to warmer, even tropical, parts of the world. Indeed, many of our most common houseplants hail from such far-flung places as the forests of Brazil, the mountains of East Africa and the foothills of the Himalayas. But they are no longer being taken from the wild, of course. To satisfy demand, such plants are being mass-produced in nurseries and being bred to produce

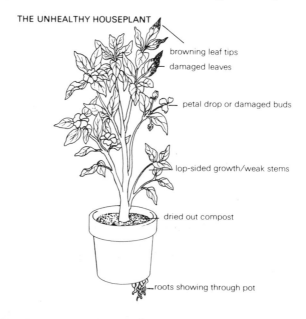

THE UNHEALTHY HOUSEPLANT

browning leaf tips

damaged leaves

petal drop or damaged buds

lop-sided growth/weak stems

dried out compost

roots showing through pot

new strains that will be better suited to the home environment. The nurseryman, therefore, is doing his bit to help the houseplant gardener – the plant will be labelled and this will include basic advice as to how it should be cared for. It won't, however, carry any guarantee of survival – that's down to you!

Bear in mind, after all, that you are expecting your houseplants to thrive in what is essentially a totally unnatural situation – apart from anything else, their roots are stuck in a pot. The secret of success, therefore, is fully to understand their requirements so that you can provide as near-ideal conditions as possible – and, because they can't fend for themselves, be willing to meet their every need.

Buying Plants

Responsibility for the well-being of your plants starts long before you carry them over the threshold. The biggest mistake is to buy a houseplant on impulse – just because it looks good – without giving a thought to its specific needs.

Obviously you want to make sure that the houseplant you are buying is healthy and the best way of doing that is to buy from a reputable garden centre or florist or from certain high-street chain stores. Beware of places selling them off the pavement – the plants will be suffering all sorts of traumas while they're sitting there – and also any shop where the display looks neglected and untidy. The main danger signals are shrivelled or yellowing leaves, weak stems, lop-sided growth, petals dropping from flowers or damaged buds and dried-out compost. It's also wise to treat with suspicion any large foliage plants with over-small or very lightweight pots.

Have a firm idea, too, of the sort of effect you want to create – a mass of frothy foliage, perhaps, or a kaleidoscope of colour; a collection of sculptural silhouettes or a soft oasis of scent. In this way you can concentrate on those plants that are best equipped to do the job and, in turn, avoid costly errors of judgement. You'll also find that the enormous selection of houseplants on the market suddenly appears slightly less overwhelming.

The following list outlines the main factors to consider when it comes to making your final choice:

- Light – does the plant need full sun/bright indirect light/shade?
- Position – is it sensitive to draughts?
- Temperature – is there a min./max. requirement and can this be kept?

- Water – are its needs critical/fairly routine?
- Air – does it want a dry/humid atmosphere? What about fumes, perhaps from a gas fire?
- Size – will it grow too big for its allocated position?
- Health – is it being cared for? Is it in a good condition?

Where to put Plants

In most homes conditions vary quite considerably from one room to another, even from corner to corner. And that means they can usually accommodate a fairly wide range of plants. It's certainly rare for a house not to be able to offer a home to at least a limited selection, even if it means sticking to shade-tolerant toughies like the aspidistra – its resilience earned it the name of 'cast-iron plant'!

The first step is to determine where you think displays of houseplants would be both effective and practical, bearing in mind that you will have to live with them. Then, theoretically, you can set about choosing plants that will be happy in the places you've earmarked. But don't start dismissing plants right, left and centre as unsuitable candidates – or, for that matter, get carried away because your enormous windowsill receives the sun all day! What might appear to be an ideal spot can often have its drawbacks and, similarly, an apparently hopeless situation can invariably be improved.

Bear in mind, too, that standing plants in serried ranks – say, on a shelf or fireplace – generally does them little justice. Far better to allow a special specimen plant to be seen in splendid isolation or to arrange plants in groups. In fact, compatible houseplants – that is, ones having exactly the same cultural requirements – can even be grown in the same container, just as long as it is large enough.

A major advantage of this type of permanent grouping is that the interaction of the plants forms a sort of micro-climate in which they can enjoy conditions more akin to those in their natural habitat. What's more, being in a permanently planted group encourages the plants to settle down and acclimatise to their surroundings – and that, incidentally, is why you should resist the temptation of continuously moving your houseplants from pillar to post. Even if a plant isn't in the very best of spots, it will very often adapt to the conditions given time. Give it a different home every other week and it won't know what's expected of it!

Assessing conditions around the house

Near a window: Light levels will vary according to the aspect. North-facing rooms can be very dark (choose shade-tolerant plants), ones facing south can be too sunny (net curtains or blinds will provide necessary shade).

Windowsills: In north-facing/dark rooms windowsills are ideal as long as there are no draughts. Unless you have double glazing, don't trap plants behind curtains at night. Windowsills are not a good idea if plants have constantly to be moved. Sunny windowsills can prove scorching, so provide shade.

Darker corners: Light levels can drop considerably just a few feet from a window. Explore the possibility of providing artificial light – there are special 'growing' bulbs that fit into ordinary sockets.

Central heating: This makes the air very dry, especially when turned up full-blast. Raise the humidity by misting plants with water, standing them on trays of gravel soaked with water, or installing a humidifier. Don't place plants right by or over radiators. Try to keep the temperature even.

Cold spots: Few houseplants will tolerate sudden chills (if by windows at night), cold draughts (if by an outside door) or prolonged low temperatures. Use unheated rooms for overwintering some tender garden plants.

RAISING HUMIDITY
mist with hand sprayer

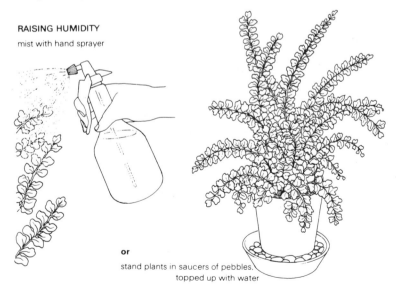

or
stand plants in saucers of pebbles,
topped up with water

Bathrooms: The steamy, humid atmosphere suits such plants as ferns and African violets. But position with care – bathwater full of compost is no joke!

Kitchens: Can be treated like any other room in the house, although delicate plants won't appreciate too many fumes (perhaps from a gas cooker). Consider making a display of herbs.

Looking After Your Plants

When and how to water

The most common fate of houseplants is death by drowning! And so the key to success, generally, is: 'If in doubt, leave it out!' The vast majority of plants like to have their feet in a compost that is kept just nicely moist. But there's no golden rule as to the frequency of watering that will achieve this – how quickly the compost dries out depends on how actively the plant is growing, the temperature in the room and the level of humidity. The answer, then, is to let the plant tell you when it needs a top-up, and you can do this as follows:

✍ The finger test: gently press a finger about 2.5 cm (1 in) or so into the compost. If it feels damp and soil particles are left clinging to your finger, it doesn't need watering.

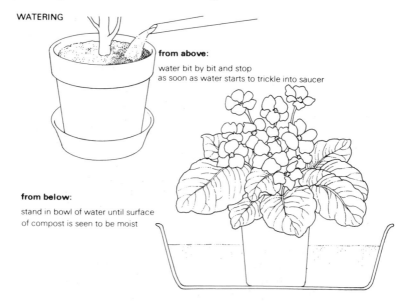

WATERING

from above:
water bit by bit and stop
as soon as water starts to trickle into saucer

from below:
stand in bowl of water until surface
of compost is seen to be moist

☛ The pot test: get to know the weight of the pot and plant when the compost is moist – as the compost dries out it will become noticeably lighter and you can safely add water.

It's always preferable to let the compost just begin to dry out between waterings rather than risk making it over-wet – unless, that is, the plant has special requirements. And bear in mind, too, that considerably less water will be needed from about October through to March when the plants are making little growth. It's important that houseplants are allowed to 'rest up' in winter, and reducing water levels is just one of the ways of encouraging this.

Most plants can be watered from above. Water a little at a time, allowing it to seep into the compost bit by bit – you can stop when water starts to trickle from the drainage holes into the saucer. If water gushes into the saucer immediately you start watering, it usually means the compost has dried out and shrunk away from the pot. If this happens, you'll have to water from below – a method also recommended for such plants as African violets and cyclamen. Place the pots in a sink or washing-up bowl of water – almost up to their rims – and leave them until you see droplets of water on top of the compost. They can then be left to drain (no pot should be allowed to sit in water) before being returned to their permanent positions.

A thought for food

Houseplants, like garden plants, take nourishment from the soil, and while the compost in the pot will be fairly rich in plant foods initially, these will soon be depleted as the plant grows. Sooner or later, then, it will be necessary to feed your houseplants with a proprietary fertiliser. These come in various guises – liquids, powders, pills and solid sticks – and, as with garden fertilisers, are fully labelled as to how they should be applied and what they will do (some are designed to encourage flowering, say, while others will stimulate foliage). More important than the form of fertiliser, though, is when and how often it should be used.

As with watering, feeding follows a seasonal cycle. When your plants start into active growth in spring, they'll need a steady supply of food to sustain them. That's the time to begin feeding, therefore, and you can continue to do so right through to about the end of September. 'Little and often' is the best plan, although you should always follow the instructions on the packet. Never feed plants during the winter months as it will stimulate unnatural growth, which will sap their strength. Nor should you feed any houseplants that are at all unwell – identify and rectify the problem first of all.

In the pot

Initially, watering, and perhaps feeding if the plant is actively growing, should be your only real concerns. For if you buy from a reputable source, the pots will be neither too big nor too small for the size
of the plants they contain and, in turn, they will hold sufficient compost to allow strong root growth. As the plants get bigger, though,
their roots inevitably outgrow their pots. That's when they start to
wind their way around the inside of the container in their search for
fresh earth and even begin to creep out through the drainage holes.
The plants have become what is commonly called 'pot-bound'.

Moving a plant into a slightly larger container (potting on) is best
done in spring, just before it wants to start into active growth. It won't
hurt to pot on at any time during the growing season but certainly
don't do it immediately before or during the plants' winter resting
period. As you will see, it's not a complicated process:

1 Have a new container ready – its diameter should be no more than
4 cm (1½ in) bigger than that of the old one. (Potting on also gives you
the opportunity to choose a different type of container. Bear in mind
that clay ones dry out more quickly than plastic. If you go for a decorative pot, make sure that it has drainage holes.)

2 Buy in a supply of pre-packed potting compost. You don't necessarily have to stick to a peat-based type (this is what houseplants are

POTTING ON

*support plant and tap side of
pot sharply to release root-ball*

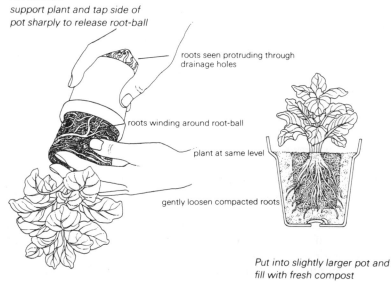

roots seen protruding through
drainage holes

roots winding around root-ball

plant at same level

gently loosen compacted roots

*Put into slightly larger pot and
fill with fresh compost*

usually sold in). The alternative would be a soil-based one, like John Innes, of which there are three formulations, Number 1, Number 2 and Number 3. The idea is to progress gradually, over a year or two, from one to the next so that the increasingly high plant-food content is matched to the plant's rate of growth and size. Number 3 is best for large plants or permanent group plantings.

3 If using clay or ceramic pots, place a few crocks (clean pebbles, broken clay tiles) over the drainage holes. Calculate how much deeper the new pot is than the old one – it shouldn't be much more than 2.5 cm (1 in) or so – and fill the new container with compost to that depth.

4 Now gently remove the plant from its pot, which is most easily done when the compost isn't too moist. Holding the pot in one hand, slip the fingers and palm of the other over the top of it – so that you can contain the compost and support the plant's stems. Turn it upside down and give the side of the pot a firm tap against, say, the edge of a table. Then ease out the pot-shaped root-ball.

5 Stand the root-ball in the new pot, making sure that the upper surface is not too low or too high – 1–2.5 cm (½–1 in) below the rim is about right.

6 Fill in the gaps around the sides – not over the top – with fresh compost and gently firm down, making sure that the root-ball isn't standing proud. Water the plant and, again, check that the compost is level.

Potting on invariably gives plants a new lease of life but it shouldn't be overdone. Some plants, in fact, seem to prefer to be slightly potbound, so check the cultural requirements of your plants first. Finally, don't be tempted to move a plant into a much bigger pot in the hope that it can then stay put and flourish for a good few years. The more compost there is, the colder and wetter will be the roots, and that's never a good thing.

Day-to-day care
While you don't want to be forever fussing over your plants and causing them undue disturbance, you should keep your eyes peeled for any tell-tale signs of stress so that you can take immediate action – for example, isolating a diseased plant so that it doesn't infect the others. Whatever the problem, the sooner it is rectified, the less permanent damage will be done. And, incidentally, if you do spot anything that looks like a pest or disease, treat all your plants – just to be on the safe side – with a proprietary insecticide or fungicide specifically designed for houseplants.

To keep your display looking neat and tidy, trim off any browning leaves (the odd one here and there is inevitable) and remove fading flowers. Make sure that climbing plants have adequate support – with a small panel of trellis or a moss pole – and keep wildly spreading plants in check by gathering up the stems within a discreet framework of plant sticks and string.

You can perk up tired-looking compost by lightly forking over the surface – a particularly good idea in winter when the plants can't be repotted – and you can clean up dusty leaves by gently wiping them with cottonwool soaked in water. This is especially beneficial when the days are getting shorter in autumn as it will enable the maximum amount of available light to penetrate the leaves.

Top Ten Houseplants

Rieger begonia (Begonia elatior *hybrid)*: This begonia was specially bred in Germany as a houseplant and as such is far better suited to conditions in the home than most other types. Given a fairly cool, light position, with plenty of humidity, it is likely to produce its waxy-like, usually red/pink flowers throughout the year.

Japanese aralia or false castor-oil plant (Fatsia japonica*)*: Grow this one for its striking, glossy-green foliage. The large, palmate leaves have up to nine pointed lobes apiece and are held almost horizontally on the gently branching stems. The plant usually remains fairly neat and compact, reaching about 1 m (3 ft) high – indeed, it's very easy to please if given cool, reasonably bright conditions.

Creeping fig (Ficus pumila*)*: This charming, small-leaved character is invaluable in that it can be encouraged either to climb or trail. Its soft green foliage is packed tight on the delicate rambling stems, which must be given free rein for full effect. It's not too fussy as to temperature but does appreciate humidity – mist regularly with water. There's a variegated version, which is slightly more demanding.

Winter jasmine (Jasminum polyanthum*)*: This is the common name you will probably find on the label of this wonderfully scented climbing houseplant, although strictly speaking the winter jasmine is a quite different garden plant (*J. nudiflorum*). The houseplant is usually bought with its delicate foliage already trained over a support hoop, although further support will be needed because it's a rampant grower if kept fairly cool but in good light. Fragrant white flowers are produced in profusion in the winter months.

Prayer plant (Maranta leuconeura *'Kerchoveana')*: Unlike most plants with vividly patterned leaves, the prayer plant won't prove unduly tricky. However, the one thing it doesn't want is direct sunlight – just give it a warm, bright position. The tightly packed, olive-green, oval leaves curl together towards night-time – hence its name – and are boldly marked with dark, uniform blotches, which accounts for its other common name, rabbits' tracks!

Boston fern (Nephrolepsis exaltata): This is one of the most reliable and showy ferns commonly sold as a houseplant. For it to give of its best, keep the plant fairly cool and constantly moist (not waterlogged!) and provide high humidity. A bathroom is an ideal site. It forms a feathery mass of fresh green leaves, each one gently arching and tapering to a point (it's also known as the sword fern).

Lemon-scented geranium (Pelargonium citrosum): This is just one of the many scented-leaved geraniums that will release their spicy, flowery or minty fragrances whenever you brush past them. While the flowers are insignificant, the foliage is quite intricately shaped and there are variegated forms. The best news of all is that they'll lap up the full sun of a south-facing window!

Sweetheart vine (Philodendron scandens): Another worthwhile climber or trailer, yet this time with bold, glossy green, heart-shaped leaves. It's a toughie of the houseplant world, putting up with a certain amount of neglect and not minding a rather dry atmosphere – ideally, though, keep it warm and moist and mist occasionally with water.

Gloxinia (Sinningia speciosa): Belonging to the same family as the African violet – that is, the gesneriads – the florid flowers of the houseplant gloxinias belie the easy-going nature of the plant. Flowering throughout the summer, the large blooms of scarlet, violet, pink or purple, some bi-coloured with white, make a superb display atop the impressive oval leaves. Keep in bright, indirect light and a warm, even temperature. Don't let the compost dry out.

Christmas cactus (Zygocactus truncatus): So named because its showy, salmon-pink flowers appear in mid-winter at the tips of the arching 'stems', which are fleshy and composed of flattened 'leaves' joined end to end – the foliage alone makes a striking display. It likes a light position, but not direct sun, and a fairly even, moderate temperature. It can be put outside in shade during the summer months.

CHAPTER 12

CALENDAR

January

January is the quietest month in the gardening calendar. There are few tasks to attend to outside and none will keep you occupied for very long – except, perhaps, the search for the first snowdrops. With little option, then, but to stay in the warmth and comfort of the house you can make the best of the situation by turning your thoughts to the year ahead and planning for flower borders and crops that will be the very best yet. To this end, send off for catalogues from seed companies/plant lists from nurseries and study them at your leisure. Reflect on the past season and consider how the flower garden could be improved (whether plants might need to be moved, say, or borders reshaped) and how the kitchen garden could be made to work more efficiently (for example, to provide a wider range of vegetables over a longer period, to avoid gluts and to fill gaps).

In the flower garden
Check the condition of any trees and shrubs planted in the autumn, making sure stakes/tree-ties are doing their job properly and that any protective plastic sheeting/netting around conifers and the like hasn't come adrift. In mild winters, if the ground isn't frozen or waterlogged, you can prepare the site for a new lawn and even carry out turfing if conditions are favourable. Order grass seed now too. Resist the temptation to mow the lawn. If you have a garden pool, stop it freezing over by floating a rubber ball in the water.

In the kitchen garden
If ground conditions are favourable, fruit trees and bushes can still be planted this month. Spray existing ones with tar oil to prevent diseases. Prune those planted in autumn if this wasn't done at the time. Early broad beans can be sown if the ground isn't wet or frozen.

Top ten jobs in January
1 Order seed catalogues and nursery lists.
2 Place orders for seeds.

3 Plan sowings for a succession of vegetables.
4 See how flower borders can be improved.
5 Check tree-ties/stakes.
6 Protect vulnerable plants from wind/rain/snow.
7 Keep borders/lawn free of plant debris and leaves.
8 Bring bulbs planted for indoor display into warmth.
9 Attend to the needs of winter-flowering pot plants.
10 Spray established fruit trees with tar oil.

February

Take advantage of the fact that there is still not a great deal to do out-side and start to prepare for the busy months ahead. March, in fact, will be really frantic, so get some of those time-consuming routine chores out of the way now – for example, cleaning pots and seedtrays, getting in supplies of compost, fertiliser and so on, sorting out tools and overhauling garden equipment.

In the flower garden
Keep borders tidy and free of debris and leaves. If the ground isn't frozen or waterlogged, it can be prepared for the planting of perma-nent ornamentals in spring (deciduous shrubs, in fact, could be planted now). An application of rose fertiliser around established plants would be much appreciated towards the end of this month and the lawn, too, can be aerated and top-dressed. Prune climbing plants such as late-flowering (July/August) clematis, wisteria and ornamental vines. If snowdrops have finished flowering and large clumps need dividing, do this now while the leaves are still green. Stored dahlia tubers and tuberous-rooted begonias can be started into growth in warmth. Feed bulbs in flower in the garden and keep watering those indoors.

Don't forget to attend to your houseplants, some of which will be making new growth – this is particularly tender, so make sure that the plants aren't getting chilled at night. Also, if the air in the room is very dry raise humidity levels around the plants.

In the kitchen garden
Inspect training wires/supports of cordon fruit trees and raspberries to ensure that they are standing up to the elements. Fruit can still be planted this month if ground conditions are suitable. Start sow-ing under cover for early crops of Brussels sprouts, cauliflower,

cabbage, leeks and lettuce. If growing broccoli or spinach, pick these on a regular basis. Towards the end of the month you can use cloches to start warming up the ground for sowing vegetables outside in March. Feed fruit trees and bushes with rose fertiliser.

Top ten jobs in February

1 Keep borders/vegetable plot neat and tidy to reduce the risk of pests and diseases.
2 Where possible, start preparing the ground for spring sowing/planting.
3 Rake, aerate and top-dress the lawn if the ground isn't frozen or sodden.
4 Give soil around ornamentals a top-dressing of rose fertiliser.
5 Prune wisteria, ornamental vines and late-flowering clematis.
6 Make early sowings of vegetables under cover in warmth.
7 Use cloches to start warming up the soil for sowing/planting.
8 Remove dahlia tubers from winter storage and start into growth.
9 Make a check-list and budget for tools, equipment, seed, plant material and so on needed for the coming season.
10 Start cleaning pots and so forth for raising plants under cover and getting containers/compost ready for patio plantings.

March

March marks the start of the gardening year although, while there is plenty to be done, sowing and planting will start in earnest only once the weather and ground conditions are favourable. It's still too early to sow anything but the hardiest of seeds outside – even in mild districts this should be done towards the end of the month – and none of the half-hardy annuals or vegetables raised under cover can be planted out until the frosts are well and truly over. Don't let the displays of bedding plants in shops and less reputable garden centres/nurseries tempt you into buying before the time is right as you may be wasting time and money.

In the flower garden

Lift and divide large clumps of herbaceous perennials (if this wasn't done in autumn) and, if ground conditions are suitable, plant bare-rooted permanent ornamentals and evergreen shrubs (these may need to be protected from wind). Assess your displays of bulbs and spring-flowering biennials (some of these might need supporting or tidying as part of their routine aftercare) and make a note as to how they might be improved for next year. Leave the foliage of bulbs to die down naturally – don't cut it off or tie it in knots. When conditions allow, sow hardy annuals outside where they are to flower and start off seeds of half-hardy annuals under cover. Final ground preparations should be made now for sowing a new lawn, while in some areas established ones can be given their first cut of the year, provided the ground isn't very wet. Make sure that the blades of the mower are at the highest setting and reduce the height of cut gradually over a period of weeks.

In the kitchen garden

Now is the last opportunity to plant fruit trees while they are still dormant. Similarly, winter pruning of tree and bush fruits and autumn raspberries should be completed before they start into growth at the end of March. Keep your eyes peeled from now on for aphids, caterpillars and any signs of disease. Vegetables can be sown outside and under cloches as soon as soil conditions allow – make use of successional sowings for summer salad crops. Sow tomato seed in pots on a warm windowsill. In mild districts start hardening off plants raised earlier under cover for planting out by the end of the month (if ground conditions are suitable). Harvest spring greens, late sprouts and winter cabbage and lift parsnips and leeks. Prepare cleared ground for sowing/planting.

Top ten jobs in March

1 Sow seed under cover for early flowers and vegetables.
2 Divide large clumps of herbaceous perennials.
3 Plant bare-rooted permanent ornamentals and fruit.
4 Prune established roses now and complete winter pruning of fruit.
5 Repot houseplants if pot-bound and give the plants a first feed – move if necessary to their 'summer' positions (out of direct sun and so on).
6 Start sowing hardy annuals/vegetables outside in favourable areas.
7 Sow tomatoes in pots indoors.
8 Give the lawn its first cut of the year.
9 If using cloches to warm up the soil, make sure that these are in position early in the month.
10 Clear the last of the 'winter' vegetables to make way for transplants.

April

You'll have covered plenty of ground, literally, by the end of April as the sowing of hardy annuals and vegetables and the planting of bare-rooted/container-grown permanent ornamentals (if this couldn't be done in March) can go full steam ahead. Everything in the garden, in fact, will be beginning to stir into action, including the less welcome occupants – namely, weeds and pests. To keep the latter under control, inspect plants on a regular basis so that you can nip them in the bud before the problem gets out of hand. Weeds can be most easily kept at bay by regular hoeing and the use of a mulch.

In the flower garden
There should be nothing to delay the sowing of hardy annuals where they are to flower – make room for them, if necessary, by clearing out any early-flowering biennials that may already be past their best. Bulbs that aren't to be left in the ground can be moved/stored once the leaves have died down. Dahlia tubers can be planted towards the end of the month and so, too, can any hardy annuals (especially sweet peas) that were raised under cover to provide a slightly earlier display. Half-hardy and tender plants in coldframes (and those on windowsills) should be gradually hardened off over the course of the month. Cut back spring-flowering shrubs once the blooms are finished and, early in the month, cut hard back such plants as buddleia and hardy fuchsia to promote healthy growth and keep the bushes within brounds. Give the lawn a boost later in the month by applying a nitrogen-rich fertiliser. If starting a lawn from scratch, now is the time to sow seed or lay turf, provided ground conditions are favourable. Clumps of pond plants can be replanted in aquatic baskets.

In the kitchen garden
Continue to sow outside seed of hardy vegetables and to make successional sowings of salad crops and so on (the latter should continue over the next few months). Plants from earlier sowings that need to be transplanted should be moved only when ground conditions are right. The thinning of seedlings will keep you on your toes, too, for the job must never be delayed. Remove cloches where no longer needed and use to warm soil elsewhere for sowing tender vegetables next month. Keep picking spring greens and broccoli. The most important job in the fruit garden is to protect blossom from sharp frosts by draping bushes/cordon trees with plastic sheeting or proprietary materials.

Top ten jobs in April

1 Complete all sowings of hardy annuals.
2 Sow hardy vegetables and make successional sowings.
3 Plant permanent ornamentals if this couldn't be done last month.
4 Start to harden off half-hardy plants raised under cover.
5 Cut back/prune early-flowering shrubs and buddleia, fuchsia.
6 Sow grass seed or lay turf for a new lawn.
7 Thin/transplant vegetables as necessary.
8 Keep ground weed-free, especially around young plants, and watch for pests and diseases.
9 Protect blossom on fruit from getting frosted.
10 Start to plan for sowings/plantings of half-hardy/tender flowers and vegetables next month.

May

May is the time to sow and plant all those half-hardy or tender flowers and vegetables that, between them, will add a blaze of colour to your borders and a tasty treat to your plate.

In the flower garden

In the last week of May you can safely plant out half-hardy annuals raised under cover and, where necessary, buy additional plants from nurseries and garden centres to make up the numbers and complete your planned display. Any gaps can still be filled by the sowing of hardy annuals. Now is the time, too, to plant up displays in containers – in tubs on the patio, windowboxes, wall pots and hanging baskets. Watering will become a daily routine when the weather is dry, especially with plants in containers, which dry out quickly and often don't benefit from even a quite heavy downpour. From May to the end of August you can sow biennials and perennials in a spare patch of ground (or in containers in an open coldframe) to have young plants for planting out in autumn. In established borders pay attention to aftercare – for example, staking, feeding, dead-heading. Evergreen subjects if not planted now are best left until autumn. The frequency of mowing should be stepping up now – probably to at least once a week – and the height of cut should be approaching its summer setting. Sowing grass seed/turfing can be carried out if this wasn't possible last month. If you've built a garden pool, make plans for plants, which are best planted in late May/June when actively growing.

In the kitchen garden
Make first sowings outside of tender crops such as French beans (protect with cloches in colder districts). Plant out tomato plants in the last week of May. Continue to thin and transplant vegetables and to make successional sowings as required. Be on the look-out for pests and take appropriate measures against slugs, birds, weeds and so on. A weak application of a general fertiliser would be appreciated by crops that are growing apace. Water well in dry spells. The main job in the fruit garden is to keep a close watch for pests and diseases, and to take immediate action.

Top ten jobs in May
1 Plant out half-hardy/tender flowering plants.
2 Plant up displays in tubs, windowboxes and so on.
3 Sow biennials and perennials from now until late summer.
4 Be ready to water in dry spells.
5 Step up mowing – little and often is the best policy.
6 Sow grass seed or lay turf for a new lawn.
7 Sow/plant out tender vegetables such as French beans.
8 Thin/transplant vegetables as soon as necessary.
9 Keep weeds down by careful hoeing/mulching.
10 Watch for pests and diseases on all garden plants.

June

You'll have your hands full this month, but since the majority of the jobs relate to aftercare, they won't seem too much like hard work. Having been well and truly bitten by the gardening bug, you'll find yourself eager to lavish those plants with all the necessary care and attention.

In the flower garden
At the beginning of the month the majority of bulbs will be ready for lifting and storing/moving now that their leaves have died down and they have had sufficient time to build up their reserves of energy for next year. Permanent ornamentals planted the previous autumn or earlier this year may need supporting (especially climbers, of course), while any biennials that are past their best and making the border look untidy should definitely be cleared (replace with bedding plants). To prevent pest and disease problems, start spraying shrubs and roses with a systemic insecticide as soon as you see signs

of attack and use a systemic fungicide to guard against mildew and blackspot. Make sure that young/newly planted subjects are kept moist at the roots by watering copiously in the evenings whenever there is a dry spell. Be ready to water the lawn, too, using a sprinkler or hose, again in the evening – in droughts, leaving the clippings on the lawn will help to retain moisture. Mowing may be necessary twice a week from now until the end of summer. If you haven't done so already, plant up the garden pond with a properly balanced selection of aquatics.

In the kitchen garden
Sow beetroot, carrots and turnips for storing. Continue with successional sowings, using them to fill gaps between long-term crops, and transplant/plant out young plants and thin seedlings as required. Keep weeds down, water well in dry weather and watch for pests and diseases, taking appropriate action – pick off caterpillars or spray plants with derris. Early crops of cabbage, cauliflower and broad beans will be ready to harvest. Now's the time to lay straw (or perforated polythene sheeting) on the ground around strawberry plants and to thin out fruits on dessert gooseberry bushes.

Top ten jobs in June
1 Make final plantings of bedding plants and tender vegetables.
2 Keep all plants in the garden well watered in dry spells. Mulch to help retain moisture in the soil.
3 Carry out routine sprayings and continue to watch for caterpillars and slugs (both can be removed by hand).
4 Attend to the aftercare of established permanent ornamentals.
5 If you want bigger roses for cutting, remove the smaller buds clustered round the central one. Feed.
6 Attend to the needs of hardy annuals – providing support for sweet peas, for example.
7 Keep up with vegetable sowings as required.
8 Harvest fruit and vegetable crops regularly.
9 Thin out gooseberry fruits and use those removed for cooking.
10 Lay straw around strawberries to protect fruits.

July

Come mid-summer, the fruits of your labours will be a joy to behold. You may even find time to sit back and congratulate yourself.

In the flower garden

Watering will be the order of the day (or evening, in fact) and special attention must be paid to plants in containers and developing young plants. It's vital to keep weeds down, too, since these will compete for any moisture that is in the soil. Keep dead-heading flowers as necessary and prune shrubs that have finished flowering (according to individual requirements). Hedges should be clipped to keep them in shape and lawns trimmed around the edges. A weak solution of nitrogen-rich fertiliser can be used to give the lawn a boost (but not if the weather is very dry or hot). Make sure that houseplants are watered regularly and give them a breather outside on fine days. Don't put them in direct sunlight.

In the kitchen garden

There's little more to sow in the vegetable plot, except cabbages for early spring next year and a few more successional sowings, especially of salad crops. Continue to see to the needs of young/developing plants – thinning, transplanting, watering, weeding, controlling pests and diseases – and harvest crops as soon as they are ready. Attend to outdoor tomatoes (staking cordons and mulching with straw/polythene under bush types) and apply a general fertiliser to all maturing crops. Pick strawberries, raspberries, currants and gooseberries as soon as they are ready and inspect developing fruits on apples and pears – if they are weighing down the branches, support the latter with strings or a wooden prop stuck in the ground. Continue routine spraying programmes. Attend to summer strawberries that have finished fruiting (remove mulch/cut back foliage and runners/feed) and also summer raspberries.

Top ten jobs in July

1 Water all contain plants on a daily basis unless there's been prolonged, heavy rain.
2 Keep borders/vegetable plot completely free of weeds.
3 Trim hedges and earlier-flowering shrubs.
4 Keep lawn edges neat and tidy and mow grass twice a week.
5 Don't forget to water/feed/mist houseplants.
6 Sow spring cabbage for an early crop next year.
7 Attend to the needs of outdoor tomatoes.
8 Harvest fruit just as soon as it is ripe.
9 See to summer strawberries and raspberries when fruiting is over.
10 Continue a spraying regime against pests and diseases.

August

The main priority in the ornamental garden is to keep the flower displays looking as fresh and tidy as possible, for while many may be coming to the end of their season, you and the family are probably only now finding the time to relax and enjoy them. The kitchen garden will keep you busy with so much to harvest/lift and store.

In the flower garden

Dead-head flowers as soon as they fade and tidy up/cut back spreading, straggly bedding plants in borders and containers. Check supports and stakes of dahlias and the like. Transplant biennials and perennials and pinch out the growing tips of young wallflower plants. Trim evergreen and conifer hedges now so that they can recover from the shock before the colder weather sets in. Continue to mow the lawn on a regular basis.

In the kitchen garden

Pay special attention to the watering of actively developing/ripening crops and harvest as soon as they are ready. Continue to thin or transplant earlier-sown vegetables as necessary and to weed around plants. Pest and disease control is still important. Attend to the training of cordon tomatoes, removing side shoots and so on. In the fruit garden leave remaining fruits to ripen on the trees/bushes – except pears, which are best ripened indoors – and protect from birds by draping with nets. Carry out summer pruning of new shoots on cordon trees. Plant strawberries for a really good crop next summer.

Top ten jobs in August

1 Dead-head, trim back and generally tidy up flower displays.
2 Transplant biennials and perennials for summer flowers next year.
3 Pinch out growing tips of young wallflower plants.
4 Give evergreen hedges their last trim of the year.
5 Continue to water in dry spells, especially ripening vegetables and fruit.
6 Harvest vegetables as soon as they are ready.
7 Leave all fruit to ripen on trees, except pears which should be picked for ripening indoors.
8 Protect fruit from birds by draping trees and bushes with netting.
9 Remove side shoots and the growing points on cordon tomatoes.
10 For maximum yields, plant strawberries at the end of the month.

September

September is one of the most rewarding months in the gardener's calendar, for while summer displays may be coming to an end, the garden is nevertheless full of colour and interest, often having an air of well-worn maturity even when only recently established.

In the flower garden
Bulb planting should be a top priority this month, both outside – in tubs, borders and lawns – and for indoor display in bowls. As displays of annuals come to an end at the end of the month, they can be cleared out so that biennials can be planted for spring/early summer colour next year. Don't lift dahlias until the foliage has been properly blackened by frost, which probably won't be for some time yet. Many herbaceous perennials will still be putting on a good show, so continue to see to their needs and also carry out any pruning that might be required by other permanent ornamentals. September is an ideal month for turfing a new lawn and while grass seed can be sown now too, it shouldn't be left any later. Reduce the frequency of mowing, gradually raising the cutting height, and apply an autumn lawn fertiliser. Prepare houseplants for their period of winter rest by cleaning the foliage, feeding less often (at reduced strength) and watering only when really necessary.

In the kitchen garden
Late-sown vegetables that have yet to ripen fully will benefit from being covered with cloches. Other crops should be harvested as soon as they are ready. Make sowings of winter radish and spinach. As sufficient ground becomes clear, dig it over, removing any plant debris and putting healthy waste material on to the compost heap (burn anything else). Continue to water and weed around growing crops and to control pests and diseases. Pick apples as required for eating/cooking. Harvest soft fruits as soon as they are ripe. Prune and train summer cane fruits and finish summer pruning of cordon trees.

Top ten jobs in September
1 Plant bulbs for display both outside and indoors (in bowls).
2 Clear borders of annuals that have finished flowering or are no longer looking their best.
3 Replace any annuals that are past their best with biennial plants (either grown from seed yourself or bought in).
4 Lay turf or sow grass seed to create a new lawn.

5 Reduce the frequency of mowing and raise the height of cut.
6 Pot on houseplants if necessary and reduce the amount of food/water.
7 Use cloches to aid the ripening of late-sown vegetables.
8 Continue to water and weed around growing crops and harvest regularly.
9 Pick soft fruit as it ripens and bottle or freeze as necessary.
10 Start to plan and make preparations for the planting of ornamental trees and shrubs next month.

October

The main priority this month is to get everything in the garden sorted out and settled in before the worst of the winter weather arrives. And the more you can do now, of course – when conditions are still quite favourable – the less you'll have to worry about when, come next February or March, the ground is still frozen or waterlogged and it's impossible to get any work done.

In the flower garden
This is a good time for planting ornamental trees and shrubs in containers. Protect the foliage of conifers and other evergreens from wind scorch and excess water loss. Herbaceous perennials may need lifting and dividing – in well-established borders it is a good idea to have a real sort-out every few years so that the ground can be thoroughly dug and manured before replanting (make sure that the plants are labelled when divided so you know what's what). If the stems and foliage of dahlias have been frosted, these can be lifted and stored. Cut back withered stems of hardy perennials. Carry out autumn pruning and tidying up of deciduous shrubs and climbers, but first check their individual requirements. Permanent ornamentals in containers should be moved to a more sheltered site and steps should be taken to improve drainage and protect them from frost. Mowing should cease by the end of the month – the last cut should be just a very light trim – and the sowing of new lawns should be completed by then too. Clear garden ponds of any decaying vegetation, cut down the foliage of marginal plants and remove submersible pumps for winter storage. In colder districts, float a rubber ball on the water to stop it freezing over and, wherever you live, cover the pool with a frame of wire netting to stop it getting clogged up with autumn leaves.

In the kitchen garden
Clear away waste vegetable debris and prepare vacant ground for the growing of vegetables next spring. Continue to harvest cabbages and early Brussels sprouts and pick the last of the runner beans and lettuce. Lift and store beetroot, turnips and carrots. Spring cabbages will be ready for transplanting – keep the ground around all winter crops free of weeds by regular hoeing. Pick and store apples and ensure that summer raspberries have had their old wood cut back and new shoots tied in to wires. Check out sources of fruit trees for planting at the beginning of next month.

Top ten jobs in October
1 Plant ornamental trees and shrubs.
2 Lift and divide large clumps of herbaceous perennials.
3 Carry out autumn pruning/tidying up of summer-flowering shrubs and climbers (according to individual requirements).
4 Protect permanent ornamentals in tubs from the worst of the elements – frost, wind, snow.
5 Aim to stop mowing the grass by the end of the month.
6 Tidy up garden ponds and protect against falling leaves.
7 Lift and store root crops (parsnips can be left in ground).
8 Clear the ground as crops finish, dig over and prepare for next spring.
9 Pick and store apples.
10 Stop feeding houseplants and let them settle down for the winter.

November

As the main growing season gradually winds down, November is the ideal month to take a critical look at your garden and assess its strengths and weaknesses. For without the distraction of so much summer colour, the bare bones of the garden will be all too obvious. Visit local parks and gardens open to the public to seek inspiration and discover which plants are putting on a really good autumn and winter show – then identify them so that you can add them to your shopping list.

In the flower garden
The planting of bulbs, and especially tulips, should be completed this month. Don't forget to plant some in bowls and plunge them in peat for bringing indoors in early spring. Bare-rooted trees and shrubs

can be planted without delay – just as long as the weather doesn't turn frosty – and late herbaceous perennials no longer flowering can have their top growth cut right down. Weed between established plants and lightly fork over the ground. Protect less hardy subjects from frost, by covering the clumps with peat and check that any tree stakes/ties, training wires, supports and so on are quite secure. Sweep fallen autumn leaves off the grass on a regular basis and, now that mowing is finished, aerate the lawn. Clean, overhaul or service any gardening equipment before storing for winter.

In the kitchen garden
The sooner fruit trees and bushes can be planted, the better – just make sure that the ground isn't wet and sticky or frozen. Remove protective netting from currant and gooseberry bushes because most birds (bullfinches are the exception) will do them more good than harm during the winter by eating up insect pests. If these bushes are several years old, they might need pruning and tidying up now. Cut back any new shoots from summer-pruned cordon apples and pears. Keep an eye on stored fruits, removing any that are ripening or deteriorating. Continue to harvest vegetables when ready or as required and to clear away remains of crops, putting healthy material on the compost heap. As long as the ground isn't sticky, digging of cleared ground can continue. Keep weeds down between winter crops.

Top ten jobs in November
1 Finish planting bulbs for outdoor and indoor displays.
2 Plant bare-rooted ornamental trees and shrubs and fruit.
3 Cut down top growth of late herbaceous perennials.
4 Protect vulnerable subjects from frost with peat.
5 Keep sweeping up fallen autumn leaves on the lawn – use to create a useful supply of leafmould.
6 Check that stakes, tree-ties, plant supports and so on are stable and secure and not causing damage to the plants.
7 Check apples and pears in store.
8 Continue to clear ground of waste material and debris when crops have finished – dig over if conditions allow.
9 Clean, overhaul and service equipment prior to winter storage.
10 Seek inspiration for effective autumn and winter planting schemes.

December

Prepare for a well-earned rest and send away for as many seed catalogues and plant lists as possible so that you can spend lazy evenings planning what you are going to grow next year. And don't forget to drop plenty of hints as to what Father Christmas might like to bring you – all sorts of tools and gadgets, many quite inexpensive, make ideal gifts and will be far more useful than all those hankies!

In the flower garden

Order seeds and plants as early as possible so as to guarantee that you get exactly what you want. If the weather is mild and ground conditions are favourable, you can prepare any new borders you might be planning for next year's displays. If you want a hedge, suitable plants can go in now. Continue to keep the lawn clear of fallen leaves and also carry out any lawn repairs, but try to keep off the grass as much as possible if it is very wet or frosted. Carry out winter pruning and tidying of permanent ornamentals that require it. For colour in the home at Christmas, buy in bowls of forced bulbs and winter-flowering pot plants – but choose these with care, otherwise they will turn out to be short-lived 'disposables'.

In the kitchen garden

Digging cleared ground and hoeing between winter crops will be the main jobs in the vegetable plot. If you're keen, broad beans can still be sown under cloches early in the month. Leeks may need earthing up now. Keep a close eye on vegetables in store, removing any that are deteriorating. Wash and sterilise all pots and seedtrays. Keep inspecting fruit in store and carry out winter pruning of trees and bushes as necessary – spraying with tar oil should follow.

Top ten jobs in December

1 Send off for seed catalogues and plant lists.
2 Start to plan for next year's flower displays and vegetables.
3 Keep leaves off the lawn.
4 Carry out winter pruning of ornamentals and fruit as necessary.
5 Buy in top-quality pot plants for Christmas flowering.
6 Inspect fruit and vegetables in store.
7 Dig over/prepare empty ground as conditions allow.
8 Keep hoeing between growing crops.
9 Drop hints in the right direction for useful Christmas presents.
10 Rest up while you have the chance!

INDEX